THE R.E.W.R.I.T.E. METHOD
WORKBOOK

The Parent and Educator Action Plan

for Getting Middle Schoolers to

Fall in Love with Writing

By

T.D. Flenaugh

ISBNs: 979-8-9887076-8-4 (Paperback)
       979-8-9887076-3-9 (eBook)

DISCLAIMER: The advice contained in this book might not be suitable for everyone. The author designed the information to present her opinion about the subject matter. The reader must carefully investigate all aspects of any decision before committing. The author obtained the information contained herein from sources she believes to be reliable and from her personal experience, but she neither implies nor intends any guarantee.

The author particularly disclaims any liability, loss, or risk taken by individuals who directly or indirectly act on the information contained herein. The author believes the advice presented here is sound, but readers cannot hold her responsible for either their actions or the risk taken by individuals who directly or indirectly act on the information contained herein.

First published in the United States of America.

Published by Writertai LLC

Printed in the United States

Cover Design by TD Flenaugh

THE R.E.W.R.I.T.E. METHOD WORKBOOK

TABLE OF CONTENTS

HOW TO USE THIS WORKBOOK

The REWRITE Workbook: The Parent and Educator Action Plan for Getting Middle Schoolers to Fall in Love with Writing serves as an inseparable companion to *The REWRITE Method: The Parent and Educator Guide for Getting Middle Schoolers to Fall in Love with Writing*. The REWRITE Workbook should be used to prepare a plan and to enact the plan with the ready-made activities within this book. I have included the essential pages to hook children into learning while filling in gaps in understanding. Eventually, children will be compelled to pursue writing interests and topics that motivate and expand their imagination, and this workbook provides activities and strategies to support children when this switch occurs. This will happen for different learners at varying stages of their writing journey.

The series of pages labeled **PARENT-EDUCATOR PAGE** were made for caregivers and teachers to explain, guide, and check possible answers. Pages labeled **Student Handout** are for learners to practice their skills. I encourage you to remix these pages and fine-tune activities to meet the needs and desires of your budding writers.

The journey towards writing love will not be easy, but it will be worth it. Consistent practice and encouragement will garner the desired results. There is no substitute for regular writing and on-time feedback that is nurturing. Measure the growth and the gains your learner is making. Use The REWRITE Workbook suggestions for tracking progress, and celebrate improvement by comparing where they started to their current writing prowess.

More in-depth support can be found by joining our community at fallinginlovewithlearning. com and through the weekly episodes of the Falling for Learning Podcast at https:// fallinginlovewithlearning.com/podcast.

Remember! Do not expect perfection from teens and tweens as they grow; do not expect it from yourself. Keep going, keep growing, keep writing!

R	RECOGNIZING TALENT & LEVEL OF PERFORMANCE	Figure out strong aspects and weak areas of their writing
E	EFFECTIVE FEEDBACK	Provide input that is viewed as constructive and comprehensible
W	WRITING PROCESS	Stages of writing - from idea generation to final draft.
R	REAL WORLD PURPOSES	Challenging children to write for specific audiences and for publications
I	INTENTIONAL PRACTICE	Setting goals and working toward writing improvement.
T	TRAITS	Naming and explaining writing qualities to establish clear expectations
E	ENCOURAGE CREATIVITY	Establish a writing practice that is driven by kids' choice and unique tasks that stimulate learners

About the R.E.W.R.I.T.E. Method

The R.E.W.R.I.TE. Method is composed of principles and concepts used to support falling in love with writing. These strategies have been built throughout my teaching and mothering experiences.

As I engaged my child, my family members, and my students in the process of developing their personal style and expressing themselves using the written word, I have figured out what works best.

Reflection: How do you usually engage your learner in writing?

_____

_____

_____

_____

_____

_____

_____

CHAPTER 1
R FOR
ROOT CAUSES
AND
RECOGNIZING TALENTS

YES. / NO

ROOT CAUSE CHECKLIST

There are many reasons why a child dislikes writing. Explore whether any of the following issues plague your child:

01 Fine motor skills: Is there a struggle with holding a pencil or pen?
YES ☐   NO ☐

02 Lack of confidence: Do they avoid writing? OR Shares a lot of ideas, but is hesitant and produces very little when it is time to write.
YES ☐   NO ☐

03 Learning differences or disabilities: Does the child have an identified learning difference or disability?
YES ☐   NO ☐

04 Lack of interest: Is the topic interesting to the child? OR Did they want to choose another topic?
YES ☐   NO ☐

05 Negative past experiences: Did the child describe negative experiences with writing?
YES ☐   NO ☐

06 Limited exposure: Has the child had limited exposure to different types of writing?
YES ☐   NO ☐

What is your child's writing level? Determination Quiz

Conventions

Conventions - <u>G</u>rammar, <u>U</u>sage, <u>M</u>echanics, <u>S</u>pelling, <u>C</u>apitalization

Does their writing follow G.U.M.S.-C. rules?

- All the time
- most of the time
- about half the time
- less than half the time
- rarely

Writing Stamina

How much can your child write in 15 minutes?

- one paragraph - six sentences or fewer
- two/three paragraphs - at least six sentences each
- four/five paragraphs - at least six sentences each

Clarity

- clear and complete sentences
- paragraphs are focused on a topic
- Vocabulary usage is accurate and appropriate

Organization

- introduction
- supporting paragraphs
- conclusion
- logical order - cause and effect, comparison, etc.

RECOGNIZING TALENTS CHECKLIST

Here are some questions to help you identify those key talents:

Spoken Expression

☐ Are they naturally funny?

☐ Do they have a knack for pointing out intriguing aspects of things in a unique way?

☐ Do they often say phrases that make them stand out?

☐ Do they incorporate advanced words into their speech?

☐ Can they describe things in a captivating way?

Handwriting

☐ Neat handwriting?

☐ Words spaced out

☐ Follows capitalization rules

Vocabulary

☐ Writing features high level vocabulary

☐ Uses humor in their writing

☐ Writing uses interesting descriptions

☐ Writing includes sensory details

Observations to Capture Writing Potential

☐ Closely observe the things they say.

☐ If necessary, jot it down.

☐ Use their spoken words as evidence to demonstrate their writing potential.

☐ Encourage them to write down their words,

☐ Repeat back to them their mastery of spoken language and knack for turning a phrase.

Notes

_____

_____

AREAS OF IMPROVEMENT

As you begin working with a child to recognize talents, areas of Improvement will also be easy to note. During this beginning phase of the REWRITE Method, do not try to address these issues. These challenges will be worked on in later phases of the program. Fight the urge to point out these issues. Use this sheet to mark what you notice.

_____

_____

_____

_____

_____

_____

_____

_____

_____

_____

_____

_____

_____

_____

CHAPTER 2
E FOR
EFFECTIVE FEEDBACK

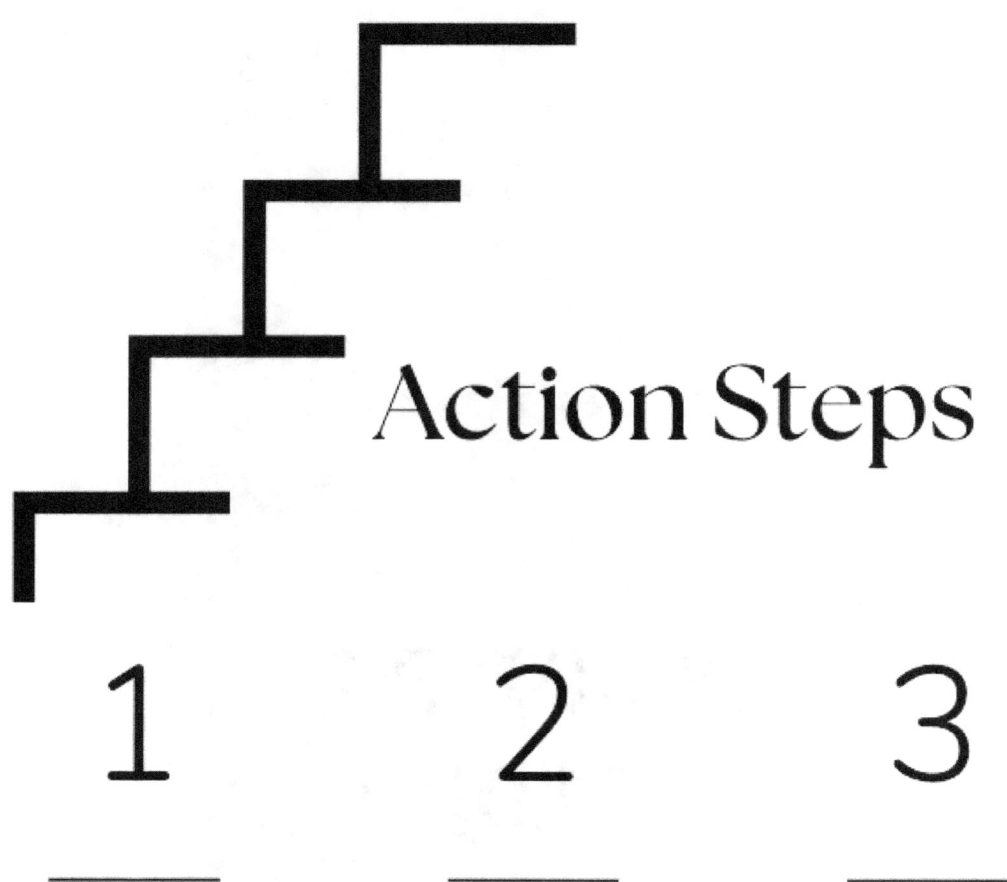

Action Steps

1
Encourage your child.

2
Change or reframe the negative messages about writing coming from you or other members of the family.

3
Try out fun activities to engage your child with writing and allow them creative license!

The R.E.W.R.I.TE. Method is composed of principles and concepts used to support falling in love with writing. These strategies have been built throughout my teaching and mothering experiences as I engaged my child, my family members, and my students in the process of developing their personal style and express themselves using the written word.

E FOR EFFECTIVE FEEDBACK

Start commenting on areas of strength, not areas that need improvement. Leading with deficits causes children to doubt their writing ability and associate writing with negativity. Start a new practice of overcomplimenting. Here are a few ways to begin even if a child's writing needs a lot of support!

HANDWRITING

"You have taken the time to write so neatly!"
"You have spaced out the words to make the writing easy to read."

ORGANIZATION

"You have started new paragraphs to organize ideas."
"You have started new page(s) to give yourself enough room to explain your ideas."

IF WRITING IS ILLEGIBLE, HAVE THEM READ ALOUD.

Ask your child to read aloud their work. Listen carefully for the flow.
"Thanks for spending time on your writing! Please read it to me!"
Take note of well-written phrases.

CREATIVITY

Applaud your child's use of descriptive details, interesting details, and funny parts.
If the writing makes you feel an emotion, comment on this positively.
"Writing that makes people react emotionally is a sign of a talented writer. This part made me feel _____."

4 POSITIVE TO 1 IMPROVEMENT RATIO

Fight the urge to fix all of their writing mistakes. To inspire young writers, compliment their work. Four positive comments should be noted before providing a suggestion for improvement.

Prepare Compliments

Even if you cannot read it, prepare a few compliments:

1. "Looks like you worked hard on this. Why don't you go ahead and read your writing to me."
2. "This is such a thoughtful gesture! Your grandma will really love this."
3. "Wow! You wrote an entire page!"
4. "I really liked when you wrote this line: (read the line). It was very _____ (touching, funny, etc.)!"

Here are a few more ideas to note areas of strength:

☐ High-level vocabulary

☐ Use of sensory details

☐ Correct capitalization.

THE ANATOMY OF MINI-LESSONS

Mini-lessons

When your child has never heard of or has limited knowledge about a concept or skill, provide a mini-lesson. Mini-lessons refer to a short (10-minute or less) sequence of activities to introduce a skill. The need for a mini-lesson also arises when someone makes the same type of mistake repeatedly, indicating confusion about a topic.

The Anatomy of a Mini-Lesson

Use the mini-lesson handout for the word *wander* and *wonder.*

1. Give them a quick explanation of the meanings.
   * Explain the concept yourself or use an instructional video to demonstrate.
2. Demonstrate how to correctly complete the task or skill.
   * Use a writing piece that exhibits the skill.
   * Model how to identify the differences between a correct and incorrect example.
3. Lift sentences from their writing by copying the sentences on a separate document, on a poster, or on a separate piece of paper. Deconstruct sentences to ensure they know how to correct them.
4. Make the learning stick. Reinforce this concept or skill by giving them practice once a week for the next month. Schedule four practices at regular intervals to facilitate committing the skill to long-term memory.

SAMPLE MINI-LESSON
(WONDER VS. WANDER)

Understanding Wonder and Wander

Teach students that "wonder" involves thoughts or emotions, while "wander" relates to physical movement without a specific direction. If students practice using these words correctly, it will enhance their writing skills!

Definitions:

Wonder: To feel curious, amazed, or in awe about something; a feeling of admiration or surprise.

Synonyms: marvel, ponder, speculate, contemplate.

Wander: To move around without a specific purpose or direction; to roam or meander.

Synonyms: roam, stroll, roam, meander.

Instructional Explanation:

"Wonder" relates to curiosity or amazement about something, while "wander" refers to movement without a particular destination or aim. Remember, "wonder" involves thoughts and emotions, while "wander" involves physical movement.

Example Sentences:

- She couldn't help but wonder about the mysteries of the universe.
- They decided to wander through the forest, enjoying the sights and sounds.

Writing Piece:

Read the following passage and see if you can infer the meanings of "wonder" and "wander" from the context:

As Emily walked along the beach, she couldn't help but wonder at the beauty of the sunset. The colors painted across the sky made her pause and admire the natural artwork. After some time, she decided to wander along the shoreline, collecting seashells and feeling the sand between her toes.

Identifying the Difference:

Wonder: Think of it as being about thoughts or emotions, often associated with curiosity or amazement.

Wander: Focuses on physical movement without a specific purpose or direction.

Deconstructing Sentences

Let's analyze these sentences from the passage:

1. "She couldn't help but wonder at the beauty of the sunset."

* *Here, "wonder" is used correctly, indicating the feeling of amazement or curiosity about the sunset's beauty.*

2. "After some time, she decided to wander along the shoreline."

* *"Wander" is correctly used here, describing Emily's aimless walking along the shoreline.*

Correct the following sentences:

1. He wandered what would happen next in the story.

   Correction: "He wondered what would happen next in the story.

2. They were wondering through the park, enjoying the scenery.

   Correction: "They were wandering through the park, enjoying the scenery.

WONDER VS. WANDER MINI-LESSON
STUDENT HANDOUT

Definitions

Wonder: To feel curious, amazed, or in awe about something; a feeling of admiration or surprise.

Synonyms: marvel, ponder, speculate, contemplate.

Wander: To move around without a specific purpose or direction; to roam or meander.

Synonyms: roam, stroll, roam, meander.

Example Sentences:

• She couldn't help but wonder about the mysteries of the universe.
• They decided to wander through the forest, enjoying the sights and sounds.

Written Piece:

Read the following passage and see if you can infer the meanings of "wonder" and "wander" from the context:

As Emily walked along the beach, she couldn't help but wonder at the beauty of the sunset. The colors painted across the sky made her pause and admire the natural artwork. After some time, she decided to wander along the shoreline, collecting seashells and feeling the sand between her toes.

Correct the following sentences. Explain why each one is incorrect.

1. He wandered what would happen next in the story.

_____

_____

2. They were wondering through the park, enjoying the scenery.

_____

_____

HOW TO REFRAME MISTAKES

☐ Be understanding of writing errors.

☐ Accept young writers at their level. (Avoid comments about what they should be doing at this age).

☐ Don't make a child's writing mistakes personally as a parent or teacher - even if they are simple mistakes. For example, don't say things like "I know I taught you that!"

☐ Instead of commanding children to redo their writing, get in the habit of asking them to read their work aloud. Then have children share what they noticed about their writing.

☐ Repair the damage of past negative feedback by over-complimenting your children.

☐ Share with them the many times you tried and failed before finally mastering different skills.

☐ Use the word revision and editing instead of describing it as "correcting" or "fixing" their work.

NOTES & IDEAS

_____

_____

_____

_____

_____

_____

_____

HOW TO PROMPT REVISION

Instead of pointing out errors or making suggestions, ask questions that suggest revision. Here are a few questions that can be asked when developing narratives or accounts of personal experiences:

1. Sounds like she had an interesting style. Tell me more about what she was wearing.
2. It sounded like you had a lot of fun at the park. Take time to explain more about it. Give three detailed sentences to describe the park. For example, describe three different areas of the park or three different types of equipment for playing.
3. What did your group do on the trip? What are three events that happened during the trip? Give us those details. I want to know more.

These suggestions for improvement do not feel critical. They show interest in the student's writing. The questions, when answered, will extend what is already written and stretch the writer toward strengthening their descriptive skills.

NOTES & IDEAS

_____

_____

_____

_____

_____

_____

_____

_____

_____

PEER REVIEW AND FEEDBACK TECHNIQUES

Team activities ignite a love for writing. Peer review happens when fellow students work together to read and review each other's work to get better at self-reflection, self-editing, and self-revision.

The REWRITE Method Peer Review Set-Up

1. Pair up two writers who will each come with a draft of their writing.
2. If the partners are new at peer review and feedback, we recommend starting with editing. Editing is the most manageable area to provide feedback.
3. Hone in on one type of error, such as capitalization. Provide them with a peer review handout
4. Provide a Peer Review Checklist to guide students through the steps.

NOTES & IDEAS

_____

_____

_____

_____

_____

_____

_____

_____

_____

_____

MORE ABOUT PEER REVIEW CHECKLISTS

A key tool for peer review is to have a checklist. Checklists can be altered based on purpose. Sometimes, the checklist may be for editing (correcting errors), or revision (improving writing quality).

Revising	Editing
☐ Word choice - specificity	☐ Capital letters
☐ Add details	☐ Spelling
☐ Transitions	☐ Sentence punctuation (run-ons)

The purpose should be narrow, such as revising for word choice to reduce repeated words. The result will be a more specific and more focused writing piece devoid of redundancies.

Procedure for the ***REWRITE Peer Review Process:*** 1. Students keep their own papers. 2. Partner A will read their paper aloud to their partner. 3. Partner B will ask Partner A questions about the partner's writing. 4. Partner A takes notes and changes their paper based on questions and suggestions from Partner B.	***Scaffolding Towards*** ***Self-editing & Revising*** Forming each word allows them to: • notice repeated words and phrases. • catch that the wording does not fit. • eventually be able to identify low quality.
Benefits of the Partner in Peer Review The partner asks questions to fill in gaps. The writer will naturally miss details because it is clear in their minds. Allow the writer to remain in control. • sit side by side with a peer • follow the checklist. • The writer should be the only one marking and making changes to their writing. • The partner gives suggestions.	***Creative Control in Peer Review*** The writer decides whether to heed the reviewer's feedback. • Writers may choose to leave their writing unchanged. • Kids must develop their voice through personal preference. • Of course, they will earn a grade or score based on meeting specific criteria.

PEER REVIEW PROCESS
STUDENT SHEET

Procedure for the REWRITE Peer Review Process

1. Students keep their own papers.

2. Partner A will read their paper aloud to their partner.

3. Partner B will ask Partner A questions about the writing.

4. Partner A takes notes and changes their paper based on questions and suggestions from Partner B.

PEER REVIEW CHECKLIST
FOCUS: CAPITALIZATION

Check for Lowercase Errors

☐ Beginning of sentences

☐ Specific names of people (i.e., Barack Obama, Beyonce Knowles, and Kamala Harris)

☐ Capitalize the names of specific places, such as restaurants, parks, streets, cities, and stores (i.e., Ladera Park, Vons Grocery, McDonalds, and Los Angeles)

☐ Capitalize the word "I"

☐ Capitalize abbreviations (after spelling out the meaning the first time, i.e., NRA for the National Rifle Association)

☐ Capitalize the name of titles (except for small words in the middle of the title like the, a, of, in, on, and the word "and")

Check for Uppercase Errors

☐ Do not capitalize general locations: a park, a store,

☐ Do not capitalize letters in the middle of words

☐ Do not use all capitals (unless it is to show emphasis)

Note the words and phrases that needed to be corrected:

_____

_____

_____

_____

_____

PEER REVIEW CHECKLIST
FOCUS: ENDING PUNCTUATION

Count the number of periods, question marks, and exclamation points in the draft

How many are there BEFORE the peer review? _____

How long is the draft? Number of lines _____

This writing piece may have many run-on sentences, which means that one sentence may continue for a long time without any punctuation, such as a period (.), a comma (,) or a semicolon (;). This means that there is more than one sentence joined together without following punctuation rules.

Tips for finding the end of the sentence:

☐ Determine a complete thought or piece of information (includes both a noun and the action or state of being).

☐ Break up the sentence between two different ideas or pieces of information that have one of the following words: and, then, next, because

☐ Remember that a simple sentence usually does not have more than one phrase with the words and, then, next, because. This means the sentence needs to have a comma and a conjunction to join two ideas. Then the sentence or run-on could also be broken down into smaller sentences or combined into compound sentences.

Note details about the sentences that needed to be corrected:

_____

_____

_____

_____

_____

PEER REVIEW CHECKLIST
FOCUS: SENTENCE STARTERS

How many sentences in the writing piece begin with the same word? _____

How many sentences are in the writing piece? _____

This writing piece may have many of the same sentence starters, which means this writing piece can be revised to add sentence variety. Once we revise your sentences, your work will flow better.

Tips for achieving sentence variety:

☐ Invert sentences by beginning with the end. For example, "Allen washed his coat because it was dirty." Inverted: Because it was dirty, Allen washed his coat.

☐ Use a pronoun or other type of description in place of the noun (the subject of the sentence).

☐ Combine short sentences.

Note the changes made to create sentence variety:

_____

_____

_____

_____

_____

_____

_____

_____

NAME:_____ DATE: _____

PEER REVIEW CHECKLIST
FOCUS: SENTENCE STRUCTURE

How many sentences are in the writing piece? _____

How many sentences in the writing piece are simple? _____

How many sentences in the writing piece are compound? _____

How many sentences in the writing piece are complex? _____

☐ My sentences are varied in structure, using different sentence types (simple, compound, complex)?

☐ I avoided or fixed run-on sentences (too many ideas strung together).

☐ I avoided or fixed sentence fragments (incomplete sentences).

☐ I appropriately used conjunctions or made edits to join sentences and ideas together.

Note the changes made to create sentence variety:

_____

_____

_____

_____

_____

_____

_____

_____

PEER REVIEW CHECKLIST
FOCUS: PARAGRAPHING FOR A NARRATIVE

Organize narratives into separate paragraphs. Check the rules for separating paragraphs in a narrative have been followed.

☐ When there is a new speaker, start a new paragraph.

☐ If there is a new location

☐ A new time of day

☐ A new day.

Note the reasons the paragraphs were separated:

_____

_____

_____

_____

_____

_____

_____

_____

_____

_____

WORD CHOICE ACTIVITY
REVISING FOR REPEATED WORDS

PART 1: *Underline the repeated phrase in the paragraph below.*

Original Paragraph (ANSWERS)

My family welcomed a new addition recently—a sweet, adorable <u>baby sister</u>! I have been waiting eagerly to meet my <u>baby sister</u>. When I first saw my <u>baby sister</u>, I was overwhelmed with joy. My <u>baby sister</u> is so tiny and delicate. Mom and Dad are taking great care of our <u>baby sister</u>. Holding my <u>baby sister</u> feels like holding a precious treasure. I love spending time cuddling with my <u>baby sister</u>. Our <u>baby sister</u> brings so much happiness into our home. I can't wait to watch my <u>baby sister</u> grow and learn new things.

In the revised paragraph below, underline the words and phrases (including pronouns) used to replace the repeated phrase in the paragraph below.

Revised Paragraph (ANSWERS)

We are all thrilled about the arrival of our <u>bundle of joy</u>—a charming addition to our family named <u>Renee Joy</u>. The moment I laid eyes on <u>her</u>, I knew she would bring immense happiness into our lives. My ***baby sister*** is such a little angel, and we're all smitten by <u>her</u> presence. With the arrival of my <u>new sibling</u>, our family feels complete. Spending time with <u>baby girl</u> fills our hearts with immense love. We cherish every moment with our adorable <u>little sister</u>. Witnessing <u>Renee Joy's</u> growth and milestones is an absolute delight.

Discussion Points:

- Variety in Description: Notice how using different terms such as "bundle of joy," "new addition to our family," "her name (Renee Joy)," and "new member of the family" changes the tone and richness of the paragraph compared to using only "baby sister." Note that baby sister is used once in the revised version.
- Impact of Varied Language: Help children reflect on how using diverse descriptions adds depth and emotional connection to the text.
- Emotional Responses: Consider how the use of different terms evokes varying emotional responses compared to repeatedly using the phrase "baby sister."

PART 2: WORD CHOICE WRITING ACTIVITY

STUDENT DIRECTIONS

Write a short paragraph (6-8 sentences) describing a new family member or pet. Use a variety of terms and phrases to express your feelings and thoughts about this new addition. Use this exercise to explore different ways of describing someone or something new in your life.

Reminder:

Varying their vocabulary can enhance their writing and evoke different emotions in readers!

**SPECIAL NOTE **

Your child may benefit from writing a draft with repeated words at first. Then help them revise by thinking of synonyms and phrases to replace the repeated words.

WORD CHOICE ACTIVITIES
REVISING FOR REPEATED WORDS
STUDENT HANDOUT

PART 1: Underline the repeated phrase in the paragraph below.

Original Paragraph

My family welcomed a new addition recently—a sweet, adorable baby sister! I have been waiting eagerly to meet my baby sister. When I first saw my baby sister, I was overwhelmed with joy. My baby sister is so tiny and delicate. Mom and Dad are taking great care of our baby sister. Holding my baby sister feels like holding a precious treasure. I love spending time cuddling with my baby sister. Our baby sister brings so much happiness into our home. I can't wait to watch my baby sister grow and learn new things.

In the revised paragraph below, underline the words and phrases (including pronouns)

used to replace the repeated phrase in the paragraph below.

Revised Paragraph

We are all thrilled about the arrival of our <u>bundle of joy</u>—a charming addition to our family named <u>Renee Joy</u>. The moment I laid eyes on her, I knew she would bring immense happiness into our lives. My baby sister is such a little angel, and we're all smitten by her presence. With the arrival of my new sibling, our family feels complete. Spending time with baby girl fills our hearts with immense love. We cherish every moment with our adorable little sister. Witnessing Renee Joy's growth and milestones is an absolute delight.

PART 2 Writing Activity

Write a short paragraph (6-8 sentences) describing a new family member or pet. Use a variety of terms and phrases to express your feelings and thoughts about this new addition. Use this exercise to explore different ways of describing someone or something new in your life.

_____

_____

_____

_____

_____

_____

_____

_____

_____

_____

_____

_____

_____

PUNCTUATION EDITING CHECKLIST
STUDENT HANDOUT

Directions: Read through your writing slowly and aloud to catch errors. Check each item on the list systematically after completing a draft and revisions.

Punctuation:

☐ Have I used proper punctuation marks (commas, periods, question marks, etc.) where necessary in sentences?

Quotation Marks and Dialogue:

☐ Have I correctly used quotation marks for dialogue and to enclose direct quotations?

Notes and Observations

_____

_____

_____

_____

_____

_____

_____

_____

_____

_____

USAGE EDITING CHECKLIST

Directions: *Read through your writing slowly and aloud to catch errors. Check each item on the list systematically after completing a draft and revisions.*

Use of Homophones:

Have I used the correct homophones in my writing?

I have checked all the following words to ensure they are used correctly:

☐ there/their/they're

☐ its/it's

☐ your/you're

☐ wander/wonder

☐ are/our

☐ hour/our

What other words are often confused in my writing?

_____

_____

_____

_____

_____

_____

_____

GRAMMAR EDITING CHECKLIST

Directions: Read through your writing slowly and aloud to catch errors. Check each item on the list systematically after completing a draft and revisions.

Subject-Verb Agreement:

☐ Subjects and verbs in sentences are matched correctly in terms of singular or plural form

Verb Tenses:

☐ The verb tenses are consistent throughout the writing. They accurately represent the timing of actions for past, present, future, etc.

Pronoun Usage:

☐ Pronouns are used accurately, clearly referring to their antecedents.

Notes and Observations

_____

_____

_____

_____

_____

_____

_____

_____

HOW RUBRICS SUPPORT CHILDREN UNDERSTANDING & SAVE TIME

- Present rubrics before the writing is completed.
- Choose the purpose to match or customize the rubric to the task
- Rubrics need to be focused on what is being taught
- Rubrics can focus on one area
- All the elements can be combined for final projects
- Gets away from "bleeding pages" or marking every mistake in the writing
- Very clear on where they can improve and what they did well

Generic Rubric

Score	Grade	
A	4	**All required elements**
B	3	**Most of the required elements**
C	2	**Some of the required elements**
D	1	**Missing most of the requirements**
F	0	**Work was not submitted or completed**

SAMPLE RUBRICS
COMPARISON ESSAY

CATEGORY	5 Excellent	4 Good	3 Fair	2 Re-Do
Introduction (Organization)	The introduction is inviting, states the main topic and give background information on the subjects. The thesis makes a claim that goes beyond the listing of similarities and differences and creates a new understanding.	The introduction is inviting, states the main topic and gives background information on the subjects. The thesis attempts to make a claim that goes beyond the listing of similarities and differences.	The introduction states the main topic but is not particularly inviting to the reader. Background information is somewhat present on the subjects. The thesis comments on similarities and differences.	There is no clear introduction of the main topic. Background information is not present or is inaccurate on the subjects. The thesis is not present. Re-Do.
Comparison points	There are (3) three clear comparison examples between the movie and the book. Tells why it matters. (includes at least one quote)	There are (2) two comparison examples between the movie and the book (includes at least one quote)	There is (1) one comparison example between the movie and the book. (includes at least one quote)	Student has not provided any comparison or provides incorrect comparison examples between the movie and the book. Re-Do.
Contrasting points	There are (3) three clear contrasting examples between the movie and the book. Tells why it matters. (includes at least one quote)	There are (2) two clear contrasting examples between the movie and the book. (includes at least one quote)	There is (1) one clear contrasting example between the movie and the book. (includes at least one quote)	Student has not provided any contrasts or provided incorrect contrasting examples between the movie and the book. Re-Do.
Conclusion	The conclusion sums up the main points of the paper and connects to the introduction. The conclusion reveals a deeper insight and does not merely regurgitate the introduction. The conclusion states the preferred subject and explains why.	This conclusion sums up some of the main points and attempts to connect to the introduction. The writer has attempted to offer insightful commentary. The conclusion states the preferred subject and explains why.	The conclusion is present, but it repeats information instead of drawing conclusions. The conclusion only states the preferred subject.	The conclusion is unclear. There is little attempt to either sum up the main points or connect to the introduction. Re-Do.

SAMPLE RUBRICS
WRITING TRAITS (PARTIAL)

CATEGORY	5 Excellent	4 Good	3 Fair	2 Re-Do
Word Choice	Writer uses vivid words and phrases that linger or draw pictures in the reader's mind, and the choice and placement of the words seems accurate, natural and not forced.	Writer uses vivid words and phrases that linger or draw pictures in the reader's mind, but occasionally the words are used inaccurately or seem overdone.	Writer uses words that communicate clearly, but the writing lacks variety, punch or flair.	Writer uses limited vocabulary that does not communicate strongly or capture reader's interest. Clichés may be present and detract from the meaning. Re-Do.
Grammar & Spelling (Conventions)	Writer makes no errors in grammar or spelling that distracts the reader from the content.	Writer makes 1-2 errors in grammar or spelling that distracts the reader from the content.	Writer makes 3-4 errors in grammar or spelling that distracts the reader from the content.	Writer makes more than 4 errors in grammar or spelling that distracts the reader from the content.
Sentence Structure	The writer has used varied and sophisticated sentence structure.	The writer has attempted to use a variety of sentence structures. There are one or two sentence fragments	The writing feels flat due to repetitive sentence structure and incomplete sentences (fragments).	The writing style is immature. There are too many incomplete sentences (fragments). Re-Do.
Capitalization & Punctuation (Conventions)	Writer makes no errors in capitalization or punctuation, so the paper is exceptionally easy to read.	Writer makes 1 or 2 errors in capitalization or punctuation, but the paper is still easy to read.	Writer makes a few errors in capitalization and/or punctuation that catch the reader's attention and interrupt the flow.	Writer makes several errors in capitalization and/or punctuation that catch the reader's attention and greatly interrupt the flow.

CHAPTER 3
W FOR
WRITING PROCESS

THE WRITING PROCESS

Explain writing as a process to children so they know there are multiple steps. Take the time to work on each stage.

1. Prewriting

To generate ideas, pre-writing usually happens before sentences and paragraphs.
- Drawing
- listing
- making notes on graphic organizers
- creating outlines

2. Drafting

Also known as a rough draft or sloppy copy. This stage involves putting ideas into sentences and paragraphs.

3. Revising

Revision involves mproving the quality of writing:
- adding details
- choosing more precise or vivid words
- rearranging sentences for clarity and flow

4. Editing

When editing, corrections are made:
- Grammatical Errors
- Usage Errors
- Mechanics (Punctuation) Errors
- Spelling Errors
- Capitalization

Kids can learn the acronym G.U.M.S - C to eventually help them edit their work independently.

5. Rewriting

After revision and editing, rewriting takes place. For kids, one rewrite is enough. Professional writers rewrite many times before their work is ready for publication.

6. Publishing

Thanks to the advances of technology, writing can be published online or using traditional paper and bound into a book.

The Writing Process has several phases. The diagram below shows the prewriting phase separated into separate parts: prewriting and planning.

PREWRITE PHASE	
Brainstorm - Unstructured	Plan - Structured
Sketch & Label Listing Circle Map	Outline Graphic Organizers Tree Map Double Bubble Map

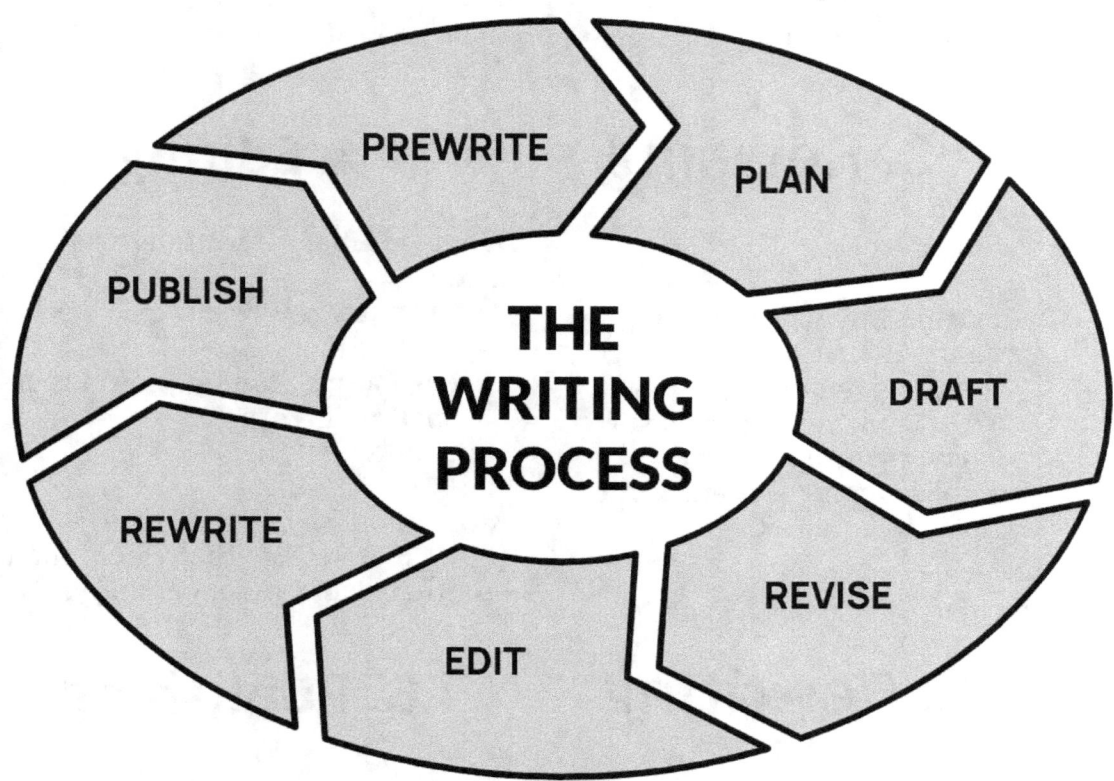

WAYS TO BEGIN THE WRITING PROCESS

The writing process is presented in a specific order, but teaches students that they could begin in different phases.

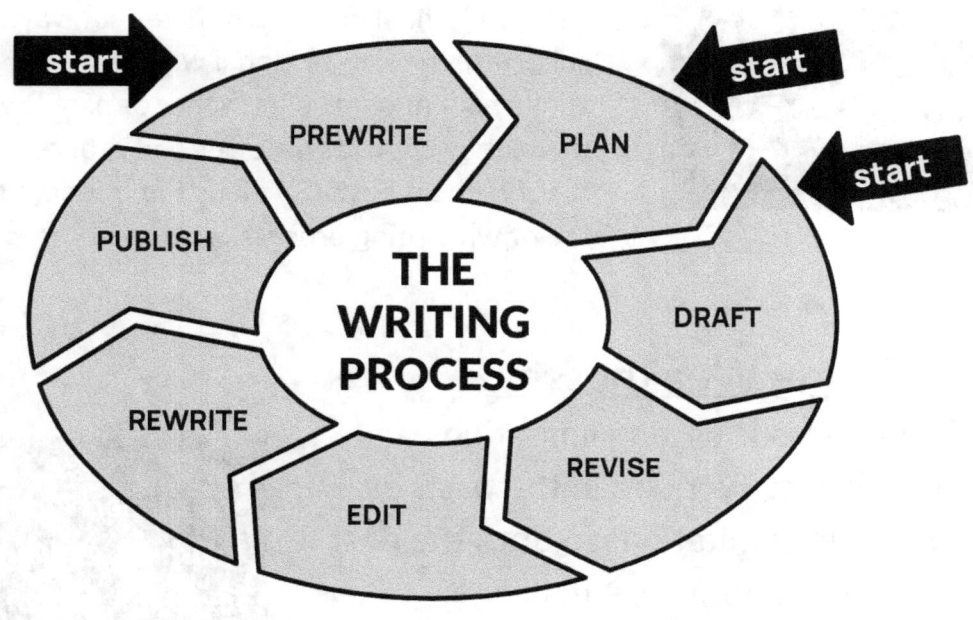

SAMPLE WAYS TO BEGIN

TOPIC: EDITORIAL AGAINST AUTOMATIC TOILETS

PREWRITE	PLAN	DRAFT
List words and phrases associated with automatic toilets	Create a tree map with three main issues with automatic toilets.	Free write different situations causing dislike for automatic toilets
Sketch pictures of issues with automatic toilets. Next label automatic toilet issues.	Write the effects of automatic toilets	Rant (or write out complaints) about automatic toilets

AN INDIVIDUAL'S WRITING PROCESS

Owning the Process

Each person will develop a writing process that is unique. Teachers present writing steps to guide students through the process, but a proficient writer gets to the final product in their own way. With your child, discuss your personal writing process. When adults no longer have a teacher or parent guiding them, they choose strategies and progress in the way that fits them best. Give kids the freedom to choose their own writing process.

> *Teachers and other adults present students with writing steps to guide youth through the process, but a proficient writer gets to the final product in their own unique way.*

Writing Weaknesses

Talk openly about your writing limitations and what you have had to work on in the past. By sharing your writing limitations in both the past and present, you will normalize making mistakes. So kids will build confidence and comfort in knowing that it is part of learning to have shortcomings. Stumbling blocks are on the path to success, and they will work on overcoming those repeated errors.

> *To support kids in learning, explain that everyone has writing weaknesses. Share your writing limitations, past and present.*

Confiding in kids about your roadblocks during your writing journey will give them confidence that they can become proficient writers.

MOVING CHILDREN THROUGH THE WRITING PROCESS

Make distinctions between the various stages. Here are a few suggestions for how to make the phases different.

PREWRITE	List ideas	Draw a picture and label it
PLAN	Create an outline for each paragraph	Use a graphic organizer that will help organize ideas (i.e., venn diagram, double double map, flow chart, cause-and-effect chart).
DRAFT	Write the rough draft by hand	Type the rough draft
REVISE	Mark up the rough draft with notes (written in a different color) to note 5 revisions that will be made.	Make a copy of the rough draft to make changes on. One copy will be the original draft. The second copy will have the revisions. OR Make notes on revisions using the comments or a different color font.
EDIT	Mark corrections in a 3rd color to note errors that need to be fixed.	Make another copy of the document and make the edits.
RE-WRITE	Type the work and include revisions and edits.	Not applicable.
PUBLISH	Require that the published version be copied into a new document with pictures.	Print work and decorate it.
	Find a location for the published version (not just for the teacher - posted on a refrigerator, emailed, framed in an office, family website or social media.	

PREWRITING ACTIVITIES
STUDENT HANDOUT

Use the space below to gather ideas about your topic. For prewriting, you do not need to write complete sentences or paragraphs. Instead think about what you will write by:

- drawing
- listing
- making notes on graphic organizers
- creating outlines

Notes and Observations

_____

_____

_____

_____

DRAFTING

☐ Use the prewrite materials (drawings, lists, notes, graphic organizers, and outlines) to form sentences and paragraphs about your topic.

☐ Make sure each idea, list, or drawing is captured in a sentence.

☐ Do not worry about spelling errors or forming perfect sentences.

☐ This is also known as a sloppy copy that only requires sentences and paragraphs in a rough form.

_____

_____

_____

_____

_____

_____

_____

_____

_____

_____

_____

THE IMPORTANCE OF REVISING

☐ This phase requires looking past the mistakes.

☐ Focus on the quality of writing.

☐ Decide on one specific way to improve the quality of writing.

☐ Remember to compliment the learner at a 4 positive to one area of improvement ratio.

To illustrate the importance of revision, consider the two sentences below:

Sentence A	Sentence B
I have a red shirt.	As I moved through the hollway, my selky scarlit blose feel smooth against my skin.
ANALYSIS	
No errors	4 errors in spelling 1 error in verb-tense (feel instead of felt)

Early elementary level vocabulary	High-level vocabulary
	  - Scarlet is sophisticated color
	  - Blouse is a specific type of shirt
	  - Sensory details (feels smooth)

Simple sentence	Complex sentence

For a middle schooler, the second sentence is more appropriate. If we were to only look at editing for errors, Sentence A would not need any further work. Sentence B would be criticized, but middle schoolers should produce sentences with grade-level vocabulary and varied sentence structures.

REVISION STUDENT SHEET

☐ Rearrange sentences to improve flow

☐ Rearrange paragraphs to improve flow

☐ Add information to make sure topic or information is clear by including sensory details, related statistics, personal connections, and connections to media or society)

☐ Delete extra or off-topic information

☐ Improve the word choice by including figurative language or specificity

Notes and Observations

_____

_____

_____

_____

_____

_____

_____

_____

_____

_____

_____

EDITING CATEGORIES

Conventions

During the editing stage of the writing process, the rough draft is checked to correct errors in the following areas:

G	GRAMMAR	Grammar has to do with following grammar rules, such as subject-verb agreement and pronoun-antecedent agreement.
U	USAGE	Are the words used correctly in context? Usage involves frequently confused words such as: wander, wonder, specific, pacific, too, to, two.
M	MECHANICS AKA PUNCTUATION	Do you see sentences that last for several lines without punctuation? Make sentence breaks. Are dialogue and cited sources punctuated correctly?
S	SPELLING	Check to see if the writing follows spelling rules.
C	CAPITALIZATION	Capitalize the beginning of sentences, proper nouns, and the pronoun I.

EDITING GUIDELINES

G	Grammar	Pronoun-antecedent agreement Correct verb-tense
U	Usage	Words are used correctly in context, including homophones, homonyms, and frequently confused words
M	Mechanics	Rules are followed for punctuation with commas, periods, and semicolons
S	Spelling	Words are spelled correctly
C	Capitalization	Capitalization rules are followed

As you spend more time working with children, these guidelines can be more specific to pinpoint the areas of growth for your particular child or children.

EDITING STUDENT SHEET

G	Grammar	Pronoun-antecedent agreement Correct verb-tense
U	Usage	Words are used correctly in context, including homophones, homonyms, and frequently confused words
M	Mechanics	Rules are followed for punctuation with commas, periods, and semicolons
S	Spelling	Words are spelled correctly
C	Capitalization	Capitalization rules are followed

Notes and Observations

_____

_____

_____

_____

_____

_____

_____

_____

_____

_____

_____

PUBLISHING CHECKLIST

☐ Lines are spaced as required (double-spaced, single-spaced, etc.)

☐ Includes pictures and images that enhance understanding of the topic

☐ Includes charts, and graphics that enhance understanding of the topic

☐ Margins meet guidelines (1 inch at top and bottom or other required measurements)

Notes and Observations

_____

_____

_____

_____

_____

_____

_____

_____

_____

_____

_____

PUTTING SCAFFOLDS IN PLACE

Remind children that scaffolds are temporary. These supports provide a bridge to meeting grade-level expectations. This chart provides suggested scaffolds to support learners in moving through the writing process successfully.

PREWRITE	Create the list of ideas with the child	Draw a picture and label it with the child.
PLAN	Give the child a partially filled-out outline for each paragraph.	
DRAFT	Scaffold by providing a document with sentence starters.	
REVISE	Give the child a focus for revision, such as word choice or sentence starters.	
EDIT	Give the child a focus for edits, such as capitalization or ending punctuation.	
RE-WRITE	Not applicable.	
PUBLISH	Not applicable.	

Inform children of their expected outcomes by the end of the unit or year. Students need to know what they are required to produce as middle schoolers. Then remind them every time the scaffold is used.

USING SENTENCE FRAMES

This scaffold involves providing children with the beginning words of a sentence. Heavy scaffolding may have up to five words so that a student only needs to add one or two words.

Heavy scaffolding

Naomi is going to the store for _____.

Medium Scaffolding

Naomi is going _____.

Light scaffolding

Naomi is _____

Notes and Observations

_____

_____

_____

_____

_____

_____

_____

_____

_____

SCAFFOLDING WITH OUTLINES

Outlines provide the paragraph-by-paragraph structure of a multiple paragraph response. Scaffold by detailing what should be the focus of each paragraph. A medium level of scaffolds can include a focus and details for the sentences in each paragraph. Heavy scaffolding may include sentence frames in the outline.

Sample Outline

MEDIUM SCAFFOLDING only provides the focus of each paragraph and a suggested topic for content in a paragraph.

1. Introduction
    a. Definition
    b. Overview of topic

2. Counterargument
    a. Explains opposing view
    b. Evidence with an opposing view
    c. Counterpoint - Shoots down the counterargument

3. Advancing Argument
    a. Claim - opinion
    b. Evidence
    c. Explains reasoning

4. Conclusion
    a. Summary
    b. Call to Action

HEAVY SCAFFOLDING EXAMPLE
SILK ROAD TRAVEL JOURNAL OUTLINE

Journal #1 -- Introduction

My name is (first name, last name) _____

I am from (name of country) _____

I am (name of culture – i.e. Chinese) _____

I'm traveling from (name of city) _____, (name of country) _____ to (name of city) _____, (name of country) _____.

I am traveling with (at least three people – first and last names should be consistent with your culture).

1) _____ relationship_____

2) _____ relationship _____

3) _____ relationship _____

4) _____ relationship _____

We are going to be trading _____ (item should be consistent with your culture).

We are hoping to get _____ in exchange.

We need this item so that we can _____

To prepare for our journey to _____ We are taking the following items with us:

1) _____ reason _____

2) _____ reason _____

3) _____ reason _____

4) _____ reason _____

HOW TO REMOVE SCAFFOLDS

Regularly inform students that the scaffolds are temporary, and slowly remove scaffolds.

Weeks 1-2	Weeks 3-4	Weeks 5-6	Weeks 7-8
Provide 4 or 5-word sentence frames	Provide 4 or 3-word sentence frames	Provide 1 or 2-word sentence frames	Provide 1-word sentence frames.
Heavy Scaffolding	**Medium Scaffolding**	**Medium to Light Scaffolding**	**Light Scaffolding**
Student writes one or two words	Student writes three or four words	Student writes four or five words	Student writes five or six words.

Finally, they will not need sentence frames any longer. Follow the same gradual removal schedule for outlines and any other supports.

CHAPTER 4
R FOR
REAL WORLD PURPOSES

PARENT AS WRITER

How do you use writing for personal use, family business, and career?

Here are a few ideas to consider:

Personal

☐ Journaling

☐ To do task lists

Family business

☐ Budget

☐ List of bills to pay

☐ Disputing a charge or fee

☐ Requesting a refund

Career

☐ Proposals to New clients

☐ Grant proposals

Explaining your writing process

_____

_____

Adjusting negative messages about writing

_____

_____

FAMILY LIFE AND WRITING

Think about a typical week in your family life. How often is writing used or could writing be used to get tasks done or to ensure clear communication? Crafting the best prompts for a child requires that you are attuned to your children's changing desires and interests. It also requires you to provide choices.

Use the list below to help you identify the multiple reasons for writing in your family life:

☐ Creating lists

    ☐ Groceries

    ☐ Errands

    ☐ jotting notes

☐ Writing journals

☐ Schedules

    ☐ Morning

    ☐ Evening

How long and when (specific times and length of time) will they spend on each task?

☐ Shower

☐ Personal hygiene (combing hair, moisturizing, or make-up)

☐ Getting dressed

☐ Breakfast

☐ Packing backpack (headphones, charger, laptop, books, folders, homework)

☐ Clothes preparation (ironing, folding, washing)

☐ Giving gifts

LETTER OF COMPLAINT
STUDENT HANDOUT

Scenario:

Your family received poor service at a restaurant, help your children compose a letter of complaint. Include:

☐ Problems with their order

☐ How the staff interacted with them

☐ Finding the names of owners or managers

☐ Address the letter to the establishment

☐ Use formal handwriting

PART 2

Proceed through the stages of the writing process. Where will you begin?

Prewrite	Plan	Draft
☐ Sketch and label drawings ☐ List ideas	☐ Form an outline ☐ Construct a graphic organizer that plans different parts of the letter	☐ In sentences and paragraphs write all your ideas about what you want to communicate about the experience

_____

_____

_____

_____

NAME:_____ **DATE:** _____

_____

_____

_____

_____

_____

_____

_____

_____

_____

_____

_____

_____

Notes and Observations - 4 Positive and 1 Area of Improvement

1. _____

2. _____

3. _____

4. _____

LETTERS OF ACCOLADES
STUDENT HANDOUT

Scenario:

The whole family has a great experience on a boat, a ship, a restaurant, or a cruise. Write a letter about all the great activities and moments shared. Take the time to send it to the supervisor, showing kids how their writing can make an impact.

Include:

☐ Notable parts or specific aspects of the order or experience that made it enjoyable

☐ How the staff interacted with them

☐ Find the names of owners or managers

☐ Address the letter to the establishment

☐ Use formal writing

PART 2

Proceed through the stages of the writing process. Where will you begin?

Prewrite	Plan	Draft
☐ Sketch and label drawings ☐ List ideas	☐ Form an outline ☐ Construct a graphic organizer that plans different parts of the letter	☐ In sentences and paragraphs write all your ideas about what you want to communicate about the experience

_____

_____

_____

NAME: _____ **DATE:** _____

_____

_____

_____

_____

_____

_____

_____

_____

_____

_____

_____

_____

Notes and Observations - 4 Positive and 1 Area of Improvement

1. _____

2. _____

3. _____

4. _____

ERRANDS

Adapt this handout to make it fit the needs of your family. It is a sample of how to create a task list. The point is for you to engage your child in writing so that you can make them feel comfortable practicing writing. It will also provide insight into your child's writing skills.

Writing Observations

☐ Do they know the spelling of all sight words or high-frequency words they should know?

Do they use correct capitalization?

☐ Do the sentences make sense?

☐ Is punctuation used?

Other details noticed about their writing:

Notes and Observations - 4 Positive and 1 Area of Improvement

1. _____

2. _____

3. _____

4. _____

ERRANDS
STUDENT HANDOUT

Scenario:

Your family is taking a **trip to the laundromat.** To ensure all washing is done and the right materials are packed, create a list.

☐ List the loads

☐ The quarters needed or money card

☐ Laundry detergent (or other cleaning agents like bleach).

A visit to the bank could require several tasks:

☐ Deposit checks

☐ Put saved coins in a counting machine

☐ Get two rolls of quarters

☐ Two money orders

☐ $200 cash for spending

☐ Transfer money to savings

☐ Order new checks

☐ Payment on a loan

Notes and Observations

1. _____

2. _____

3. _____

4. _____

NOTE WRITING

Notes are a delightful way to engage children in learning to write better. Try a few of these reasons to write notes to and with children to establish back-and-forth communication.

☐ Send encouragement

☐ Have a good day

☐ Positive affirmations

☐ Reminders to themselves

☐ Reminders to others

☐ Reminder to take medication

☐ To submit an assignment

☐ To ask a teacher about their scores or other information

Where to put notes:

☐ Lunchbox

☐ Backpack

☐ Pocket

☐ Purse

OTHER WRITING TASKS PLANNING PAGE

Choose writing prompts for children that have a particular audience (a specific person or group who will read or need the final product) - real or imaginary. Authentic audiences solidify the need for writing.

SAMPLE PROMPT:

Write for 15 minutes continuously to produce multiple paragraphs.
Choose one of the following topics:

☐ Write about your favorite sport or activity for a sports magazine.

☐ Write about your favorite artist (musician, music group, content creator, writer, etc.) for a music magazine.

☐ Free choice:

Write about a topic of your choice to be published in a magazine of your choosing.

_____

_____

_____

_____

_____

_____

_____

_____

ADVICE LETTERS - PLANNING SHEET

Think of an issue that the child or children have dealt with in the past. List three ideas below:

_____

_____

_____

_____

_____

_____

Planning Questions

What is an authentic structure for them to compose?

Find a printed magazine or online publication that students can write-like. What part of the real-world writing can they mimic or what parts should they make their own? Take notes below.

_____

_____

_____

_____

_____

_____

_____

ADVICE LETTER
STUDENT HANDOUT

Write an advice letter to a local newspaper or a blog to offer advice about different situations:

Advise a younger child on an issue that you have had to deal with in the past. Many life happenings help us mature and grow even though we may not realize it at first. Now that you have been through this situation, what details would have helped you while you were going through it? Write down three situations that caused you to grow.

_____

_____

_____

_____

Read the article about an ordeal. What are five details that can be helpful for someone who will deal with a similar experience?

_____

_____

_____

_____

Write a draft of an advice letter similar to the one you read. Your draft will include details about your experience.

_____

_____

_____

_____

MIMICRY - PLANNING PAGE

Have kids mimic published writers. We know that too much formulaic writing sucks the joy out of composing, and we want kids to enjoy expressing themselves through writing. Use a line from a popular poem or story as a frame. Change the subject matter to creatively discuss your child's chosen topic. Allowing kids to write about what interests them is an important part of this activity.

Suggested List of Notable Writers to Mimic:

- Renee Watson
- Toni Morrison
- Langston Hughes
- Nikki Giovanni

There is a lesson in Chapter 7 of this workbook that uses inspiration from Nikki Giovanni's poem "Ego-Tripping: There May Be a Reason Why".

_____

_____

_____

_____

_____

_____

_____

_____

_____

LEVERAGE THE LOVE FOR ARGUMENT - PLANNING PAGE

Think of a recurring debate or disagreement your child may have with you. This can also be something that they need to be reminded of on a regular basis. Write down a few ideas below:

_____

_____

_____

_____

_____

Forming personal views is part of growing up. Allow adolescents to wrestle with controversial issues and opposing viewpoints. Grant them the space to explore those ideas without shame. *Suggestions for controversial topics to explore with your child:*

☐ Abortion	☐ The age of adulthood	☐ Age to begin dating
☐ Drinking alcohol	☐ Candidates for public office	
☐ Immigration	☐ Critical race theory	

SOCIAL MEDIA FOR BUSINESS PURPOSES

Social media is integral in academic and business networking. It is essential to have children use social media beyond forging friendships.

Here are a few ideas:

☐ Contact colleges and universities to follow up on reports and get expert opinions.

☐ Writing reviews on Yelp and Google

☐ Writing movie reviews on Rotten Tomatoes or their own website

☐ Writing album or music reviews on popular websites or their own platform

Writing as Confidant

☐ The writing journal or diary can function as a confidant if they use it to…

☐ Write down complicated or emotional ideas

☐ Reflect on their decisions

☐ Think through issues and "hormotions" (a mixture of hormones and emotions)

Modeling Journal Entries

Think of how you can model journaling for students. Choose an issue that you feel comfortable sharing. Maybe a colleague is doing something disingenuous or rude. Write about how to deal with it on a professional level.

Include:

☐ Background information on the issue

☐ How you have dealt with it in the past

☐ What you wish you could have done

☐ The consequences of not being professional

☐ How you decided to handle it instead

Journals as Evidence of Growth

☐ Include the date on journal entries

☐ In the future, use it as evidence of success. They got through rough times before and can persevere again.

☐ Creates a habit of turning to or confiding in their writing.

☐ Track their progress (academic, social, sports-related, or in any area they want to improve).

WORDS AS GIFTS

When kids create gifts with words and ideas that come from their minds, they are more genuine than when we buy store-bought gifts to give. Written gifts come from children - straight from their hearts. This practice also motivates children to be of service to loved ones - to reciprocate love. Supply beautiful paper, make glitter, put designs, and allow them to design messages.

Here are some ideas:

☐ Poems

☐ Stories

☐ Cards

Identify a child's areas of interest. What makes them tick right now? Understand that a child's interests change over time. As they move into new eras of their lives, update what they like and what they do not like. It may be increasingly more difficult to figure out. They may not be as expressive as they were when they were younger. Here are a few ideas:

☐ A new law - explaining why it is unfair or fair

☐ Highlighting an injustice

☐ A petition to demand fair treatment or action

☐ Reflecting on conflicts

☐ Thinking through dilemmas

☐ Letter of appreciation to grandparents or a community member

CHAPTER 5
I FOR
INTENTIONAL PRACTICE

GOAL-SETTING WORKSHEET

First and Last Name:_____

Date: _____

A. Types of Goals:

Brainstorm or list ideas for different types of goals in each category:

1. Academic Goals:

- Improve grades in a specific subject
- Complete homework on time
- Study for tests regularly

2. Organizational Goals:

- Keep a tidy study space
- Improve time management skills
- Organize school materials effectively

3. Social-Emotional Goals:

- Improve communication with peers
- Develop better self-confidence
- Manage stress and emotions better

4. Other Goals:

- Develop a new hobby or skill
- Exercise regularly
- Learn a new language

Circle the Goal You Will Work Towards Achieving.

B. S.M.A.R.T. Goal Section:

Write your S.M.A.R.T. goal for the selected category:

1. Specific:	
2. Measurable:	
3. Achievable:	
4. Relevant:	
5. Time-Bound:	

C. Action Plan:

Outline the steps needed to achieve your goal, including dates and times to work on it:

Action Steps	Dates & Times

D. Reward for Reaching the Goal:

Decide on a reward for yourself when you achieve your goal:

Reward: _____

Parent/Caregiver Agreement:

I, _____ (Parent/Caregiver's Name), support my child in achieving their goal and agree to assist and encourage them as needed.

Parent/Caregiver's Signature: _____

Student Agreement:

I, _____ (Student's Name), commit to working on my goal and will put in my best efforts to achieve it.

Student's Signature: _____

Monthly Planner

MONDAY	TUESDAY	WEDNESDAY	THURSDAY	FRIDAY	SATURDAY

Notes:

_____

_____

_____

WEEKLY PLANNER

MONDAY	
TUESDAY	
WEDNESDAY	
THURSDAY	
FRIDAY	
SATURDAY	
SUNDAY	

TEAM ACTIVITIES

Collaborating with others can be highly beneficial in improving writing skills. One key advantage is the natural incentive to communicate. Thinking together creates a genuine reason to talk. Kids can leverage the recursive thinking, listening, writing, and speaking processes. Recursive means the cycle repeats, occurring over and over.

Writing is an extension of thinking, and working with others sparks creativity and strengthens thinking muscles because students will be processing the information continuously. Ultimately, kids will produce more robust completed written projects.

Collaborative writing activities and exercises

There are many ways to create a collaborative project or text. Joint writing activities and exercises are great tools for developing writing skills, promoting teamwork, and fostering creativity. Caregivers can write with their children, or a pair or group of kids can write together. Ideas for fun and engaging writing projects can include:

Writing a story with alternating narrators. A narrative with two main characters may have portions from alternating viewpoints. Odd chapters can be in one character's voice and even chapters in the other character's voice. This activity allows each writer to bring their unique perspective to the story, creating a dynamic narrative that will keep readers engaged. Alternating chapters or sections between different characters can help each writer explore the story from different angles and develop their own voice and writing style.

TWO-VOICE POEMS

Explore differing roles in a family, school, classroom, or team.	Each writer on the team can contribute the same number of lines, allowing them to express their ideas while expanding on each other's work.	Encourage teamwork and collaboration while developing language and communication skills.

MULTIPLE SETTING/WORLDS

- Create a story with multiple settings or worlds - The final product can feature one author's writing in one location, and the other author's work in an alternative universe.	- This activity allows each writer to create their unique setting or world, adding depth and complexity to the story. - Together, writers create a rich account, providing a fun and engaging reading experience.

TWO SIDES OF AN ISSUE

Writing partners can present two sides of an issue in their editorial to promote critical thinking and argumentation skills.	The team can construct solid arguments for both sides through discussion and reflection.
By presenting both sides, writers can learn to consider multiple perspectives and develop thorough, evidence-based argumentative pieces.	This activity advances writing skills essential for academic success.

KEYBOARDING SKILLS

Some adults think younger generations are digital natives who may not benefit from learning the basic typing skills of yesteryear.	Research supports learning to type formally. - Children may be hindered if they do not understand how to position their hands and type from the home row.
Have kids progress through a typing program that builds accuracy and speed to at least 40 words per minute.	It will… - increase the speed of getting their work done - Support navigating the digital world

TESTING PREPARATION

Type of test	Benefits	Format
☐ Name of the test ☐ Test structure ☐ Weaknesses ☐ Content assessed	College credit Private school acceptance Scholarships	**Writing tools** **Time** **Amount of reading** **Amount of writing**

BUILD STAMINA

- Start with short bursts
- Give teens and tweens a small amount of time, and make it engaging. Try to get them to a point where they want to continue, but stop anyway.
- Tell them, "You know what, we are out of time. Let's do more tomorrow." Keep them wanting more.
- Work them up to one-hour writing sessions once per month to prepare them for the demands of a test.

CHAPTER 6
T FOR
WRITING TRAITS

Writing traits are fundamental characteristics that contribute to the quality of written work. They encompass elements like organization, word choice, voice, sentence fluency, ideas, and conventions.

Writing Traits

C	CONVENTIONS	When considering G.U.M.S.C., how correct is the writing?
O	ORGANIZATION	When considering the order of sentences and paragraphs, does the writing follow a logical order or specific thinking process?
W	WORD CHOICE	When considering vocabulary, check for appropriate words (too easy, too difficult, or unfamiliar) for the audience. Are specific words used? Formal or informal?
I	IDEAS	Are there enough ideas to make the writing clear? Is background knowledge provided? Are there enough sensory details or elaboration strategies?
S	SENTENCE FLUENCY	Is there sentence variety regarding sentence lengths and types (simple, compound, complex, and compound complex)? Various sentence starters?
V	VOICE	Does the personal style shine through the writing, which can be displayed through unique phrasing, word choice, and flow of writing.
P	PRESENTATION	How is the writing published (aloud, printed, published online) or presented (on website, on paper, in a book)?

CONVENTIONS

The rules for grammar, usage, mechanics, spelling, and capitalization refer to the conventions. During the editing phase of the writing process, mistakes found should be corrected. Use the chart below to support student understanding. G.U.M.S.C. is an acronym that children can commit to memory to support independence during the editing process.

G	GRAMMAR	Grammar has to do with following grammar rules, such as subject-verb agreement and pronoun-antecedent agreement.
U	USAGE	Are the words used correctly in context? Usage involves frequently confused words such as: wander, wonder, specific, pacific, too, to, two.
M	MECHANICS AKA PUNCTUATION	Do you see sentences that last for several lines without punctuation? Make sentence breaks. Are dialogue and cited sources punctuated correctly?
S	SPELLING	Check to see if the writing follows spelling rules.
C	CAPITALIZATION	Capitalize the beginning of sentences, proper nouns, and the pronoun I.

ORGANIZATION

During the writing process, the organization takes place during prewriting by constructing an outline or a graphic organizer that separates topics into different paragraphs.

Narrative Structure

Teach children Freytag's Pyramid when writing narratives: beginning, middle, and end. The specifics of a story structure include exposition, inciting incident, rising action, climax, falling action, and resolution.

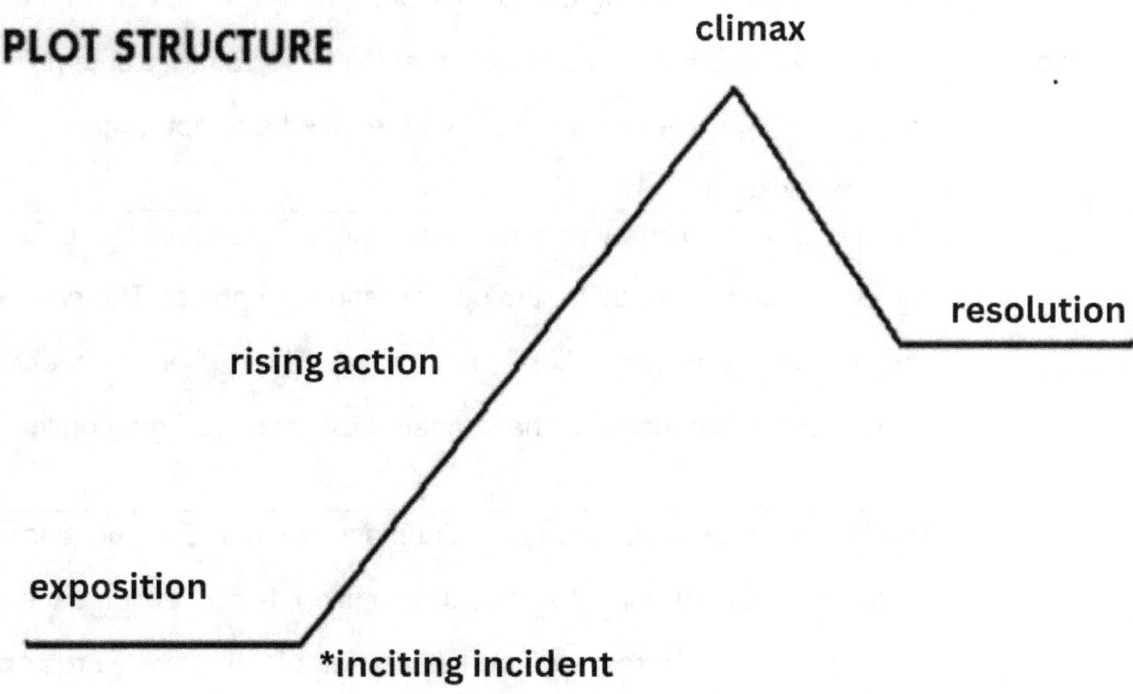

PLOT STRUCTURE

climax

resolution

rising action

exposition

*inciting incident

A well-structured event sequence refers to the narrative plot structure that includes exposition, inciting incident, rising action, climax, falling action, and resolution.

Exposition	The exposition introduces the main characters, the conflict, and the setting.
Inciting Incident	This is an event that sets the main plot in motion (like the spark that starts a fire) and introduces a conflict that the main character must face.
Rising Action	The rising action involves characters trying and failing to solve the conflict presented during the exposition. A well-developed rising action includes at least two trial attempts that fail to solve the problem. This causes more problems as a result of the failed attempt. In other words, the plot thickens.
Climax	The climax is also known as the turning point. The character or characters can finally solve the central issue or conflict. The climax usually has the most emotion in a narrative. The audience cheers for the character because they have finally won or solved the conflict.
Falling Action	The falling action addresses the minor issues caused by the rising action (or failed attempts to solve the conflict). Rising action causes more problems as a result of the failed attempts. In other words, the plot thickens. After the climax (solving the central conflict or turning point), extra problems created by the failures during the rising action are undone. Think about Harry Potter; earlier in one of the plots, one character's hand lost all muscle. That issue reverses after solving the central conflict.
Resolution	Resolution is how the characters live after the story ends. Many narratives end with "happily ever after". In other stories, the resolution explains the happenings from that point onward.

Outlines

To organize an essay or a narrative, create an outline to plan for each part or paragraph of the writing piece. Below is an example of a generic argument essay.

Argument Essay Outline

Paragraph #1	Personal Anecdote (two-sentence short story) Thesis
Paragraph #2	Reason#1 Explain reasoning Evidence (quote) Paraphrase Elaboration strategy Paragraph conclusion
Paragraph #3	Reason #2 Explain reasoning Evidence (quote) Paraphrase Elaboration strategy Paragraph conclusion
Paragraph #4	Conclusion Paragraph Restate thesis Explain major reasons Add a sentence about the future concerning this issue.

WORD CHOICE
EXPLORING FIGURATIVE LANGUAGE - DESCRIBING WOODSY SCENES

Introduction:

In literature, writers often use figurative language to paint vivid pictures and evoke emotions in their descriptions. Let's delve into three passages describing scenes in the woods, focusing on the use of onomatopoeia, metaphor, and simile. Afterward, you'll have the chance to create your own descriptive scene using figurative language.

Passage 1: Onomatopoeia

Directions: Underline the words that are examples of onomatopoeia in the following passage.

The woods buzzed and hummed with life. Bees darted from flower to flower, their wings zipping through the air. Birds chirped in harmony while leaves rustled with each passing breeze, creating a symphony of natural sounds.

Discuss with learners: Onomatopoeia is used here to mimic the sounds of bees buzzing and wings zipping, engaging the reader's auditory senses and creating a lively atmosphere.

Passage 2: Metaphor

Directions: Underline the words that are examples of metaphor in the following passage.

The woods were a canvas, with trees standing tall like paintbrushes dipped in shades of green. Sunlight streamed through the foliage, its shadows were dancers moving across the forest floor.

Discuss with learners: Metaphor is employed here to liken the woods to a canvas, trees to paintbrushes, and shadows compared to dancers offering a visual and imaginative description.

Passage 3: Simile

Directions: Underline the words that are examples of simile in the following passage.

The woods were as silent as a library at midnight. Each step on the carpet of fallen leaves echoed like whispers among the trees. The stillness enveloped the surroundings like a comforting blanket.

<u>Discuss with learners</u>: Simile is used here to compare the silence of the woods to a library at midnight and the stillness to a comforting blanket, heightening the imagery and sensory experience for the reader.

Create Your Own Beach Scene Using Figurative Language:

Imagine a scene set on a beach, and write a paragraph (6-8 sentences) using either onomatopoeia, metaphor, or simile to vividly describe the setting. Consider how you can use figurative language to evoke a specific mood or sensation in your scene.

Feel free to use the following sentence starters or create your own:

- On the beach,..."
- The beach (or the sand) was like/as..."
- The sounds of the ocean were..."
- The waves ...

WORD CHOICE
EXPLORING FIGURATIVE LANGUAGE - DESCRIBING WOODSY SCENES
STUDENT HANDOUT

Passage 1: Onomatopoeia

Directions: Underline the words that are examples of onomatopoeia in the following passage.

The woods buzzed and hummed with life. Bees darted from flower to flower, their wings zipping through the air. Birds chirped in harmony while leaves rustled with each passing breeze, creating a symphony of natural sounds.

Passage 2: Metaphor

Directions: Underline the words that are examples of metaphor in the following passage.

The woods were a canvas, with trees standing tall like paintbrushes dipped in shades of green. Sunlight streamed through the foliage, its shadows were dancers moving across the forest floor.

Passage 3: Simile

Directions: Underline the words that are examples of simile in the following passage.

The woods were as silent as a library at midnight. Each step on the carpet of fallen leaves echoed like whispers among the trees. The stillness enveloped the surroundings like a comforting blanket.

Create Your Own Beach Scene Using Figurative Language

Imagine a scene set on a beach, and write a paragraph (6-8 sentences) using either onomatopoeia, metaphor, or simile to vividly describe the setting. Consider how you can use figurative language to evoke a specific mood or sensation in your scene.

_____

_____

_____

_____

_____

_____

_____

_____

_____

_____

_____

_____

_____

_____

EXPLORING FIGURATIVE LANGUAGE - DESCRIBING CASTLE SCENES

Introduction:

Figurative language breathes life into descriptions, making them vivid and engaging. In this activity, explore how personification is used to describe scenes in a castle. Afterward, create your own descriptive scene using these literary devices.

Passage 1: Personification

Directions: Underline the words and phrases that show personification

The ancient stones of the castle whispered secrets of bygone eras, each tower and corridor bearing witness to centuries of history. The wind embraced the walls, murmuring tales of valor and intrigue as if the castle itself were recounting its own legends.

Discuss with learners: Personification is employed here to attribute human-like qualities to the castle and the wind, allowing the castle to "whisper secrets" and the wind to "murmur tales," adding depth and character to the setting.

Create Your Own Woodsy Scene Using Figurative Language

Imagine a scene set in a museum and write a paragraph (6-8 sentences) using personification, to vividly describe the setting. Consider how this literary device can bring the forest scene to life.

Feel free to use the following sentence starters or create your own:

- The leaves…
- The trees whispered secrets as if…

EXPLORING FIGURATIVE LANGUAGE - DESCRIBING SCENES STUDENT HANDOUT

Passage 1: Personification

Directions: Underline the words and phrases that show personification

The ancient stones of the castle whispered secrets of bygone eras, each tower and corridor bearing witness to centuries of history. The wind embraced the walls, murmuring tales of valor and intrigue as if the castle itself were recounting its own legends.

Create Your Own Woodsy Scene Using Figurative Language

Imagine a scene set in a museum and write a paragraph (6-8 sentences) using personification, to vividly describe the setting. Consider how this literary device can bring the forest scene to life.

_____

_____

_____

_____

_____

_____

_____

_____

_____

REVISING WRITING FOR SPECIFICITY

Part A: Writing Traits and Word Choice

1. Writing Traits:

Writing traits are specific qualities or characteristics that contribute to the effectiveness and quality of writing. These traits provide a framework for assessing and improving different aspects of written work. They encompass various elements such as organization, voice, word choice, sentence fluency, ideas, and conventions.

2. Word Choice Trait:

Word choice refers to the deliberate selection of specific words and phrases to convey precise meanings and create desired effects in writing. It involves using vocabulary that is appropriate, varied, vivid, and engaging to enhance the reader's understanding and evoke specific emotions or imagery.

Example Sentence

Sentence 1 (General Description): She wore a nice outfit to the party.

Sentence 2 (Specific Description): She donned a stylish ensemble with vibrant colors, pairing a crimson silk blouse with emerald-green trousers, accentuated by a statement necklace and sleek stiletto heels for the party.

Part B: Revision Exercise - Describing Food

Original Paragraph:

> The plate of food looked really good. It had a good taste and was good to eat. The flavors were good and it was a good mix of ingredients. Overall, it was a good meal.

Directions: In the revised paragraph below, underline the word or words that replaced the word "good" in the Original Paragraph.

Revised Paragraph:

> The plate of food appeared appetizing, boasting vibrant flavors and a delightful taste. It offered a tantalizing blend of spices, with a hint of sweetness complementing the savory ingredients. In essence, it provided a gratifying and flavorful dining experience.

Part C: Describing a Cleaned Home

Original Paragraph:

The home looked really good after the cleaning. Everything was good, from the floors to the countertops. The windows were good, and the bathrooms sparkled. All in all, it was a good job cleaning.

Chart for Specific Words:

Instead of "Good", use Specific Descriptions	
Sparkling	Floors shining
Fresh-scented	

Instructions: Revise by writing a 10-sentence paragraph that eliminates the word "good" and uses specific descriptions to highlight the cleanliness of different parts of the home.

_____

_____

_____

_____

_____

_____

_____

_____

IDEAS

These activities introduce middle schoolers to the use of sensory details in descriptions. By analyzing the provided passages, students can understand how sensory elements enhance descriptive writing. The creative exercise encourages them to craft their own descriptive scenes using visual, sound, or touch sensory details, fostering their ability to create immersive settings through sensory imagery.

SENSORY DETAILS IN DESCRIBING CASTLE SCENES

Introduction:

Sensory details are essential in bringing a setting to life in writing. In this activity, explore how visual, sound, and touch sensory details are used to describe scenes in a castle. Afterward, you'll have the opportunity to create your own descriptive scene using these sensory elements.

Passage 1: Visual Sensory Details

Directions: Underline the sensory details in each sentence. Be ready to discuss the effect of the sensory language.

The castle's grand halls were adorned with ornate tapestries, depicting scenes of valor and royalty. Stained glass windows cast colorful hues across the marble floors while towering portraits of past rulers lined the walls. Their watchful eyes seemingly followed every movement.

Discuss with learners: Visual sensory details focus on what can be seen, describing the tapestries, stained glass windows, marble floors, and portraits, creating a vibrant and rich visual image of the castle.

Passage 2: Sound Sensory Details

Directions: Underline the sensory details in each sentence. Be ready to discuss the effect of the sensory language.

Within the castle, the echoes of footsteps resonated against the stone walls, creating a symphony of reverberations. The distant clang of armor being polished mingled with the soft melodies played by minstrels in the courtyard, filling the air with a harmonious blend of sounds.

Discuss with learners: Sound sensory details immerse the reader in the auditory experience of the castle, highlighting the echoes of footsteps, the clang of armor, and the melodies of the minstrels, evoking a sense of the bustling atmosphere within.

Passage 3: Touch Sensory Details

Directions: Underline the sensory details in each sentence. Be ready to discuss the effect of the sensory language.

As one traversed the castle's corridors, the cool touch of the ancient stone walls provided a comforting solidity. Intricately carved wooden doors greeted fingertips with their smooth surfaces, while the plushness of velvet tapestries invited a gentle caress.

Discuss with learners: Touch sensory details focus on the tactile experiences within the castle, describing the sensation of touching the stone walls, wooden doors, and velvet tapestries, adding texture and depth to the description.

Create Your Own Museum Scene Using Sensory Details

Imagine a scene set in a museum and write a paragraph (6-8 sentences) using visual, sound, or touch sensory details to vividly describe the setting. Consider how these sensory elements can immerse the reader in the castle scene by appealing to their senses.

SPECIAL NOTE:

Only provide sentence starters if you think your learner needs it. Remember that these should only be used as a temporary scaffold.

Feel free to use the following sentence starters or create your own:

- In the gallery, I could see...
- The sounds within the museum were like...
- Touching the museum bench felt...

SENSORY DETAILS IN DESCRIBING CASTLE SCENES
STUDENT HANDOUT

Introduction:

Sensory details are essential in bringing a setting to life in writing. In this activity, we'll explore how visual, sound, and touch sensory details are used to describe scenes in a castle. Afterward, you'll have the opportunity to create your own descriptive scene using these sensory elements.

Passage 1: Visual Sensory Details

Directions: Underline the sensory details in each sentence. Be ready to discuss the effect of the sensory language.

The castle's grand halls were adorned with ornate tapestries, depicting scenes of valor and royalty. Stained glass windows cast colorful hues across the marble floors, while towering portraits of past rulers lined the walls, their watchful eyes seemingly following every movement.

Passage 2: Sound Sensory Details

Directions: Underline the sensory details in each sentence. Be ready to discuss the effect of the sensory language.

Within the castle, the echoes of footsteps resonated against the stone walls, creating a symphony of reverberations. The distant clang of armor being polished mingled with the soft melodies played by minstrels in the courtyard, filling the air with a harmonious blend of sounds.

Passage 3: Touch Sensory Details

Directions: Underline the sensory details in each sentence. Be ready to discuss the effect of the sensory language.

As one traversed the castle's corridors, the cool touch of the ancient stone walls provided a comforting solidity. Intricately carved wooden doors greeted fingertips with their smooth surfaces, while the plushness of velvet tapestries invited a gentle caress.

Create Your Own Museum Scene Using Sensory Details

Imagine a scene set in a museum and write a paragraph (6-8 sentences) using visual, sound, or touch sensory details to vividly describe the setting. Consider how these sensory elements can immerse the reader in the castle scene by appealing to their senses.

_____

_____

_____

_____

_____

_____

_____

_____

_____

_____

_____

These activities introduce middle schoolers to the use of taste, smell, and touch sensory details in describing riverside scenes. Students can understand how sensory elements enhance descriptive writing by analyzing the provided passages. Moreover, the creative exercise encourages them to craft their own descriptive scenes using taste, smell, or touch sensory details, fostering their ability to create immersive settings through sensory imagery.

IDEAS
SENSORY DETAILS IN DESCRIBING A RIVERSIDE SCENE

Introduction:

Sensory details play a crucial role in making a scene come alive in writing. In this activity, explore how taste, smell, and touch sensory details are used to describe scenes beside a riverside. Afterward, create your own descriptive scene using these sensory elements.

Passage 1: Taste Sensory Details

Directions: Underline the sensory details in each sentence. Be ready to discuss the effect of the sensory language.

As I sat by the riverside, the tangy taste of salt lingered on my lips, carried by the gentle breeze from the nearby sea. The occasional mist from the water sprayed lightly, leaving a faint briny flavor that mingled with the sweetness of the wild berries I snacked on.

Discuss with learners: *Taste sensory details evoke a sense of taste, describing the tangy saltiness carried by the breeze and the sweet flavors of wild berries, creating a sensory experience for the reader.*

Passage 2: Smell Sensory Details

Directions: Underline the sensory details in each sentence. Be ready to discuss the effect of the sensory language.

The riverside air was perfumed with the earthy scent of damp soil, mixed with the fragrant blossoms of nearby flowers. The distinct aroma of pine trees intermingled with the freshness of the flowing water, creating a symphony of scents.

Discuss with learners: *Smell sensory details focus on the olfactory experiences, describing the earthy scent of soil, fragrant blossoms, pine trees, and the freshness of the flowing water, transporting the reader into the setting through various scents.*

Passage 3: Touch Sensory Details

Directions: Underline the sensory details in each sentence. Be ready to discuss the effect of the sensory language.

The cool touch of the river's breeze brushed against my skin, carrying with it a refreshing chill. The soft grass beneath my feet provided cushiony support as I sat on the moss-covered rocks, feeling the smoothness of their surfaces.

<u>Discuss with learners:</u> *Touch sensory details emphasize tactile sensations, describing the cool breeze, the sensation of sitting on the grass, and feeling the smoothness of moss-covered rocks, adding texture and depth to the description.*

Create Your Own Riverside Scene Using Sensory Details

Imagine a scene by a riverside and write a paragraph of 6-8 sentences using taste, smell, or touch sensory details to vividly describe the setting. Consider how these sensory elements can immerse the reader in the riverside scene by appealing to their senses.

SPECIAL NOTE:

Only provide sentence starters if you think your learner needs it. Remember that these should only be used as a temporary scaffold.

Feel free to use the following sentence starters or create your own:

- By the riverside, I could taste...
- The air near the river smelled like...
- Touching the elements by the river felt...

IDEAS
SENSORY DETAILS IN DESCRIBING A RIVERSIDE SCENE
STUDENT HANDOUT

Passage 1: Taste Sensory Details

Directions: *Underline the sensory details in each sentence. Be ready to discuss the effect of the sensory language.*

As I sat by the riverside, the tangy taste of salt lingered on my lips, carried by the gentle breeze from the nearby sea. The occasional mist from the water sprayed lightly, leaving a faint briny flavor that mingled with the sweetness of the wild berries I snacked on.

Passage 2: Smell Sensory Details

Directions: *Underline the sensory details in each sentence. Be ready to discuss the effect of the sensory language.*

The riverside air was perfumed with the earthy scent of damp soil, mixed with the fragrant blossoms of nearby flowers. The distinct aroma of pine trees intermingled with the freshness of the flowing water, creating a symphony of scents.

Passage 3: Touch Sensory Details

Directions: *Underline the sensory details in each sentence. Be ready to discuss the effect of the sensory language.*

The cool touch of the river's breeze brushed against my skin, carrying with it a refreshing chill. The soft grass beneath my feet provided cushiony support as I sat on the moss-covered rocks, feeling the smoothness of their surfaces.

Create Your Own Riverside Scene Using Sensory Details

Imagine a scene by a riverside and write a paragraph of 6-8 sentences using taste, smell, or touch sensory details to vividly describe the setting. Consider how these sensory elements can immerse the reader in the riverside scene by appealing to their senses.

_____

_____

_____

_____

_____

_____

_____

_____

_____

_____

_____

_____

_____

These activities help middle schoolers understand how sensory details related to taste, smell, and touch can be conveyed without explicitly using those words. By analyzing provided passages, students can grasp how writers evoke sensory experiences indirectly. Additionally, the creative exercise encourages them to craft their own descriptive scenes using sensory details without explicitly stating taste, smell, or touch, fostering their ability to create vivid imagery through subtle sensory cues.

IDEAS
SENSORY DESCRIPTIONS OF A RIVERSIDE SCENE (WITHOUT USING "TASTE," "SMELL," OR "TOUCH")

Introduction:

Sensory details enrich descriptive writing by engaging readers' senses. In this activity, explore how writers use descriptions related to taste, smell, and touch without explicitly mentioning these words in a scene by a riverside. Afterward, create your own descriptive scene using sensory details.

Passage 1: Sensory Details - Taste

Directions: *Underline the sensory details in each sentence. Be ready to discuss the effect of the sensory language.*

As the gentle breeze swept across the riverside, I savored the briny tang carried from the nearby sea. The air held a hint of salt, reminiscent of ocean spray, while the wild berries I plucked emitted a sweetness that tingled on my lips.

Discuss with learners: Although not explicitly mentioning "taste," the passage evokes the sense by describing the briny tang from the sea and the sweetness of wild berries that tingled on the lips.

Passage 2: Sensory Details - Smell

Directions: *Underline the sensory details in each sentence. Be ready to discuss the effect of the sensory language.*

By the riverside, the air was rich with the earthy aroma of damp soil, mixed with the sweet scent of blossoming flowers. The pungent scent of pine trees mingled with the fresh, crisp fragrance of the flowing water.

<u>Discuss with learners</u>: While avoiding the word "smell," the passage effectively describes the sensory experience by focusing on the earthy aroma of soil, the sweet scent of blossoms, the pungent scent of pine trees, and the fresh fragrance of water.

Passage 3: Sensory Details - Touch

Directions: *Underline the sensory details in each sentence. Be ready to discuss the effect of the sensory language.*

Sitting near the river, the gentle breeze caressed my skin, carrying a refreshing coolness. The ground beneath me was soft, providing a comfortable cushion, while the smoothness of the moss-covered rocks offered a sense of tranquility.

<u>Discuss with learners</u>: Without explicitly mentioning "touch," the passage conveys tactile sensations by describing the breeze caressing the skin, the soft ground as a comfortable cushion, and the smoothness of moss-covered rocks.

Create Your Own Woodsy Scene Using Sensory Details (Without Using "Taste," "Smell," or "Touch")

Imagine a forest scene and write a paragraph (6-8 sentences) using sensory details related to taste, smell, or touch without explicitly using these words. Consider how these sensory elements can immerse the reader in the riverside scene without directly naming the senses.

SPECIAL NOTE:

Only provide sentence starters if you think your learner needs it. Remember that these should only be used as a temporary scaffold.

Feel free to use the following sentence starters or create your own:

- In the woods, the air held a hint of...
- As I sat at the base of a tree, I noticed...

IDEAS
SENSORY DESCRIPTIONS OF A RIVERSIDE SCENE
(WITHOUT USING "TASTE," "SMELL," OR "TOUCH")
STUDENT HANDOUT

Introduction:

Sensory details enrich descriptive writing by engaging readers' senses. In this activity, explore how writers use descriptions related to taste, smell, and touch without explicitly mentioning these words in a scene by a riverside. Afterward, create your descriptive scene using sensory details.

Passage 1: Sensory Details - Taste

Directions: Underline the sensory details in each sentence. Be ready to discuss the effect of the sensory language.

As the gentle breeze swept across the riverside, I savored the briny tang carried from the nearby sea. The air held a hint of salt, reminiscent of ocean spray, while the wild berries I plucked emitted a sweetness that tingled on my lips.

Passage 2: Sensory Details - Smell

Directions: Underline the sensory details in each sentence. Be ready to discuss the effect of the sensory language.

By the riverside, the air was rich with the earthy aroma of damp soil, mixed with the sweet scent of blossoming flowers. The pungent scent of pine trees mingled with the fresh, crisp fragrance of the flowing water.

Passage 3: Sensory Details - Touch

Directions: Underline the sensory details in each sentence. Be ready to discuss the effect of the sensory language.

Sitting near the river, the gentle breeze caressed my skin, carrying a refreshing coolness. The ground beneath me was soft, providing a comfortable cushion, while the smoothness of the moss-covered rocks offered a sense of tranquility.

THE R.E.W.R.I.T.E. METHOD WORKBOOK

Create Your Own Woodsy Scene Using Sensory Details (Without Using "Taste,"

"Smell," or "Touch")

Imagine a forest scene and write a paragraph (6-8 sentences) using sensory details related to taste, smell, or touch without explicitly using these words. Consider how these sensory elements can immerse the reader in the riverside scene without directly naming the senses.

_____

_____

_____

_____

_____

_____

_____

_____

_____

_____

_____

_____

_____

_____

NOTE TO PARENT-EDUCATORS

Using the following sensory details handout, provide an exemplar text to analyze how the five senses are used by the writer. Have children write-like the model (or exemplar text) to help them practice creating high level writing.

Sensory Details

sight

hear

taste

touch

smell

S FOR SENTENCE FLUENCY
COMBINING SENTENCES I

Introduction

Combining sentences can make your writing more engaging and cohesive. One way to combine simple sentences into compound sentences is by using coordinating conjunctions, often remembered with the acronym F.A.N.B.O.Y.S. Each letter stands for a coordinating conjunction: For, And, Nor, But, Or, Yet, So. By using these conjunctions with a comma, you can merge simple sentences to create compound sentences, adding depth and complexity to your writing.

Part A: Self-Driving Vehicles - Paragraph 1 (Consisting of all simple sentences)

Self-driving vehicles use advanced technology. They can navigate roads without human intervention. These cars employ sensors and algorithms. They detect surroundings to make driving decisions. Self-driving cars aim to enhance safety. Many companies are investing in this technology. Tesla and Waymo are notable examples. They offer semi-autonomous and autonomous features. Autonomous vehicles have sparked debates. They might revolutionize transportation.

Revising for sentence structure variety

Directions: Revise paragraph 1, combine at least six sentences to have a variety of simple, complex, and compound sentences

Sample Answer:

Self-driving vehicles use advanced technology. They can navigate roads without human intervention, and the cars can employ sensors and algorithms to detect surroundings and make driving decisions. Since they are aimed at enhancing safety, they are investments for numerous companies. Tesla and Waymo are notable examples, and they offer both semi-autonomous and autonomous features. Autonomous vehicles have sparked debates about their potential to revolutionize transportation.

Part B: Electric Vehicles - Paragraph (Simple Sentences)

Electric vehicles (EVs) are becoming increasingly popular. They use electric motors for propulsion. These cars produce zero emissions. EVs offer a sustainable transportation option. Many major car manufacturers produce electric vehicles. Companies like Tesla, Nissan, and Chevrolet have electric models. Charging stations for EVs are expanding. They allow convenient recharging. Some governments offer incentives for buying electric cars. Electric vehicles contribute to reducing pollution. The future of transportation seems electric.

Directions for Students

1. Underline at least 4 sentences that can be combined.
2. Revise the paragraph to include a variety of simple and compound sentences.

Revision Directions

Combine the underlined sentences using coordinating conjunctions (F.A.N.B.O.Y.S.) and commas to create a paragraph that includes a mix of simple and compound sentences, maintaining coherence and flow.

Sample Answer Revised Paragraph (Part B)

Electric vehicles (EVs) are becoming increasingly popular, using electric motors for propulsion and producing zero emissions. Many major car manufacturers produce electric vehicles, and companies like Tesla, Nissan, and Chevrolet have electric models. Charging stations for EVs are expanding, allowing convenient recharging, while some governments offer incentives for buying electric cars, contributing to reducing pollution. Consequently, the future of transportation seems electric, offering a sustainable and promising shift towards environmental consciousness.

COMBINING SENTENCES I
STUDENT HANDOUT

Introduction

Combining sentences can make your writing more engaging and cohesive. One way to combine simple sentences into compound sentences is by using coordinating conjunctions, often remembered with the acronym F.A.N.B.O.Y.S. Each letter stands for a coordinating conjunction: For, And, Nor, But, Or, Yet, So. By using these conjunctions with a comma, you can merge simple sentences to create compound sentences, adding depth and complexity to your writing.

Part A: Self-Driving Vehicles - Paragraph 1 (Consisting of all simple sentences)

Self-driving vehicles use advanced technology. They can navigate roads without human intervention. These cars employ sensors and algorithms. They detect surroundings to make driving decisions. Self-driving cars aim to enhance safety. Many companies are investing in this technology. Tesla and Waymo are notable examples. They offer semi-autonomous and autonomous features. Autonomous vehicles have sparked debates. They might revolutionize transportation.

Revising for sentence structure variety

Directions: Revise paragraph 1, and combine at least six sentences to have a variety of simple, complex, and compound sentences.

_____

_____

_____

_____

_____

_____

Part B: Electric Vehicles - Paragraph 2 (Simple Sentences)

Directions - Underline at least 4 sentences in Paragraph 2 that can be combined.

Electric vehicles (EVs) are becoming increasingly popular. They use electric motors for propulsion. These cars produce zero emissions. EVs offer a sustainable transportation option. Many major car manufacturers produce electric vehicles. Companies like Tesla, Nissan, and Chevrolet have electric models. Charging stations for EVs are expanding. They allow convenient recharging. Some governments offer incentives for buying electric cars. Electric vehicles contribute to reducing pollution. The future of transportation seems electric.

Revision Directions

Combine the underlined sentences using coordinating conjunctions (F.A.N.B.O.Y.S.) and commas to create a paragraph that includes a mix of simple and compound sentences, maintaining coherence and flow.

_____

_____

_____

_____

_____

_____

_____

_____

_____

_____

COMBINING SENTENCES II

Introduction

Combining sentences can make your writing more engaging and cohesive. One way to combine simple sentences into compound sentences is by using coordinating conjunctions, often remembered with the acronym F.A.N.B.O.Y.S. Each letter stands for a coordinating conjunction: For, And, Nor, But, Or, Yet, So. By using these conjunctions with a comma, you can merge simple sentences to create compound sentences, adding depth and complexity to your writing.

Part A: Self-Driving Vehicles

Paragraph 1 (Consisting of all simple sentences)

Self-driving vehicles use advanced technology. They can navigate roads without human intervention. These cars employ sensors and algorithms. They detect surroundings to make driving decisions. Self-driving cars aim to enhance safety. Many companies are investing in this technology. Tesla and Waymo are notable examples. They offer semi-autonomous and autonomous features. Autonomous vehicles have sparked debates. They might revolutionize transportation.

Paragraph 2 (Combining Sentences)

Revision of Paragraph 1 with combined sentences

Directions: Revise the paragraph to ensure that at least six sentences are combined to create compound and complex sentences.

Part B: Electric Vehicles - Paragraph (Simple Sentences)

Electric vehicles (EVs) are becoming increasingly popular. They use electric motors for propulsion. These cars produce zero emissions. EVs offer a sustainable transportation option. Many major car manufacturers produce electric vehicles. Companies like Tesla, Nissan, and Chevrolet have electric models. Charging stations for EVs are expanding. They allow convenient recharging. Some governments offer incentives for buying electric cars. Electric vehicles contribute to reducing pollution. The future of transportation seems electric.

Directions for Students

1. Underline at least 4 sentences that can be combined.
2. Revise the paragraph to include a variety of simple and compound sentences.

Revision Directions

Combine the underlined sentences using coordinating conjunctions (F.A.N.B.O.Y.S.) and commas to create a paragraph that includes a mix of simple and compound sentences, maintaining coherence and flow.

Sample Answer Revised Paragraph (Part B)

Electric vehicles (EVs) are becoming increasingly popular, using electric motors for propulsion and producing zero emissions. Many major car manufacturers produce electric vehicles, and companies like Tesla, Nissan, and Chevrolet have electric models. Charging stations for EVs are expanding, allowing convenient recharging, while some governments offer incentives for buying electric cars, contributing to reducing pollution. Consequently, the future of transportation seems electric, offering a sustainable and promising shift toward environmental consciousness.

COMBINING SENTENCES II
STUDENT HANDOUT

Introduction

Combining sentences can make your writing more engaging and cohesive. One way to combine simple sentences into compound sentences is by using coordinating conjunctions, often remembered with the acronym F.A.N.B.O.Y.S. Each letter stands for a coordinating conjunction: For, And, Nor, But, Or, Yet, So. By using these conjunctions with a comma, you can merge simple sentences to create compound sentences, adding depth and complexity to your writing.

Part A: Self-Driving Vehicles- Paragraph 1 (Consisting of all simple sentences)

Self-driving vehicles use advanced technology. They can navigate roads without human intervention. These cars employ sensors and algorithms. They detect surroundings to make driving decisions. Self-driving cars aim to enhance safety. Many companies are investing in this technology. Tesla and Waymo are notable examples. They offer semi-autonomous and autonomous features. Autonomous vehicles have sparked debates. They might revolutionize transportation.

Directions: Revise the paragraph to combine at least six sentences to create compound and complex sentences.

_____

_____

_____

_____

_____

_____

_____

Part B: Electric Vehicles - Paragraph (Simple Sentences)

Electric vehicles (EVs) are becoming increasingly popular. They use electric motors for propulsion. These cars produce zero emissions. EVs offer a sustainable transportation option. Many major car manufacturers produce electric vehicles. Companies like Tesla, Nissan, and Chevrolet have electric models. Charging stations for EVs are expanding. They allow convenient recharging. Some governments offer incentives for buying electric cars. Electric vehicles contribute to reducing pollution. The future of transportation seems electric.

Directions for Students

1. Underline at least 4 sentences that can be combined.
2. Revise the paragraph to include a variety of simple and compound sentences.

Revision Directions

Combine the underlined sentences using coordinating conjunctions (F.A.N.B.O.Y.S.) and commas to create a paragraph that includes a mix of simple and compound sentences, maintaining coherence and flow.

_____

_____

_____

_____

_____

_____

_____

_____

SIMPLE, COMPOUND, AND COMPLEX SENTENCES I

Part I: Introduction

Understanding different sentence structures is crucial in writing. Let us explore three main types:

- Simple Sentence: Consists of one independent clause, expressing a complete thought.
- Compound Sentence: Combines two or more independent clauses using coordinating conjunctions (F.A.N.B.O.Y.S) or semicolons.
- Complex Sentence: Contains an independent clause and at least one dependent clause, connected by subordinating conjunctions.

Part II: Combining Simple Sentences

You can turn simple sentences into compound sentences by using coordinating conjunctions (For, And, Nor, But, Or, Yet, So) with a comma or by transforming them into complex sentences by adding subordinating conjunctions (e.g., although, because, while, since).

Part A: Social Media - Paragraph 1 (Simple Sentences)

Social media platforms are popular. Many people use them daily. Users connect with friends and family. They share photos and updates. Social media allows instant communication. It influences opinions and trends. Advertisers use it for marketing. Some people spend too much time on social media. Cyberbullying is a concern. Privacy issues arise.

Directions for Students

1. Underline at least 6 sentences that can be combined.
2. Revise the paragraph to include a variety of simple, complex, and compound sentences.

Sample Answer - Revision of Paragraph 1 with Combined Sentences

Social media platforms are immensely popular as many people use them daily to connect with friends and family. Sharing photos and updates enables instant communication, influencing opinions, and trends. They also serve as a marketing tool for advertisers. Despite its benefits, some individuals spend excessive time on social media, leading to concerns about cyberbullying and privacy issues.

Part B: Hybrid Vehicles - Paragraph (Simple Sentences)

Hybrid vehicles combine an internal combustion engine with an electric motor. They reduce fuel consumption. Hybrids produce fewer emissions than conventional cars. Many car manufacturers produce hybrid models. Companies like Toyota and Honda are leaders in hybrid technology. Hybrid cars use regenerative braking. This technology recharges the battery. Hybrid vehicles offer improved fuel efficiency. Drivers enjoy cost savings on fuel. Government incentives promote hybrid adoption. The future of transportation might involve more hybrids.

Directions for Students

1. Underline at least 6 sentences that can be combined.
2. Revise the paragraph to include a variety of simple, complex, and compound sentences.

Revision Directions

Combine the underlined sentences to create a paragraph that includes a mix of simple, complex, and compound sentences, using coordinating conjunctions or subordinating conjunctions to enhance sentence structure and coherence.

Sample Answer - Revised Paragraph

Hybrid vehicles, which combine an internal combustion engine with an electric motor, reduce fuel consumption and produce fewer emissions than conventional cars. Many car manufacturers, including leaders in hybrid technology like Toyota and Honda, produce hybrid models, utilizing regenerative braking to recharge the battery and offer improved fuel efficiency, resulting in cost savings for drivers. With government incentives promoting hybrid adoption, the future of transportation might significantly involve more hybrids, marking a shift towards greener and more sustainable options.

SIMPLE, COMPOUND, AND COMPLEX SENTENCES I
STUDENT HANDOUT

Part I: Introduction

Understanding different sentence structures is crucial in writing. Let's explore three main types:

- Simple Sentence: Consists of one independent clause, expressing a complete thought.
- Compound Sentence: Combines two or more independent clauses using coordinating conjunctions (F.A.N.B.O.Y.S) or semicolons.
- Complex Sentence: Contains an independent clause and at least one dependent clause, connected by subordinating conjunctions.

Part II: Combining Simple Sentences

You can turn simple sentences into compound sentences by using coordinating conjunctions (For, And, Nor, But, Or, Yet, So) with a comma or by transforming them into complex sentences by adding subordinating conjunctions (e.g., although, because, while, since).

Part A: Social Media - Paragraph 1 (Simple Sentences)

Social media platforms are popular. Many people use them daily. Users connect with friends and family. They share photos and updates. Social media allows instant communication. It influences opinions and trends. Advertisers use it for marketing. Some people spend too much time on social media. Cyberbullying is a concern. Privacy issues arise.

Directions for Students

1. Underline at least 6 sentences that can be combined.
2. Revise the paragraph to include a variety of simple, complex, and compound sentences.

_____

_____

_____

_____

Part B: Hybrid Vehicles - Paragraph (Simple Sentences)

Hybrid vehicles combine an internal combustion engine with an electric motor. They reduce fuel consumption. Hybrids produce fewer emissions than conventional cars. Many car manufacturers produce hybrid models. Companies like Toyota and Honda are leaders in hybrid technology. Hybrid cars use regenerative braking. This technology recharges the battery. Hybrid vehicles offer improved fuel efficiency. Drivers enjoy cost savings on fuel. Government incentives promote hybrid adoption. The future of transportation might involve more hybrids.

Directions for Students

1. Underline at least 6 sentences that can be combined.
2. Revise the paragraph to include a variety of simple, complex, and compound sentences.

Revision Directions

Combine the underlined sentences to create a paragraph that includes a mix of simple, complex, and compound sentences, using coordinating or subordinating conjunctions to enhance sentence structure and coherence.

_____

_____

_____

_____

_____

_____

_____

_____

_____

SIMPLE, COMPOUND, AND COMPLEX SENTENCES II

Part I: Introduction

Understanding different sentence structures can improve the richness and flow of your writing. There are three main types of sentences: simple, compound, and complex.

- Simple Sentence: Contains one independent clause AND expresses a complete thought.
- Compound Sentence: Contains two or more independent clauses, often joined by a coordinating conjunction and a comma.
- Complex Sentence: Contains an independent clause and one or more dependent clauses, usually joined by subordinating conjunctions.

Part II: Combining Simple Sentences

To create compound sentences, join simple sentences using coordinating conjunctions (F.A.N.B.O.Y.S.) and a comma. For complex sentences, incorporate subordinating conjunctions (e.g., although, because, when) to join independent and dependent clauses.

Part A: Social Media - Paragraph 1 (Simple Sentences)

Social media platforms connect people globally. They allow sharing thoughts, photos, and videos. Users can interact in real-time. Social media facilitates communication. Many platforms are available for different purposes. Facebook is popular for networking. Instagram focuses on visual content. Twitter limits posts to 280 characters. TikTok is known for short-form videos. YouTube is a hub for video content.

Directions for Students

1. Underline at least 6 sentences that can be combined.
2. Revise the paragraph to include a variety of simple, complex, and compound sentences.

Sample Answer - Revision of Paragraph 1 with Combined Sentences

Social media platforms connect people globally, which allows the sharing of thoughts, photos, and videos. This facilitates real-time interaction and communication, and numerous platforms serve different purposes. Facebook is popular for networking; Instagram focuses on visual content. While Twitter limits posts to 280 characters, TikTok is known for short-form videos. YouTube serves as a hub for various video content.

Part B: Hybrid Vehicles - Paragraph (Simple Sentences)

Hybrid vehicles combine gasoline engines with electric motors. They aim to reduce fuel consumption. These cars use regenerative braking. This system recovers energy. It stores it in the battery. Many people opt for hybrids. They prioritize eco-friendly transportation. Hybrid cars have lower emissions. Some models switch between electric and gas power. Manufacturers like Toyota produce hybrid models. These vehicles are gaining popularity. They offer improved fuel efficiency. Some governments offer incentives.

Directions for Students

1. Underline at least 6 sentences that can be combined.
2. Revise the paragraph to include a variety of simple, complex, and compound sentences.

Revision Directions

Combine the underlined sentences to form compound or complex sentences. Use coordinating conjunctions (F.A.N.B.O.Y.S.) with commas for compound sentences and subordinating conjunctions to create complex sentences.

Sample Answer - Revised Paragraph

Hybrid vehicles combine gasoline engines with electric motors, and they aim to reduce fuel consumption. These cars use regenerative braking, which causes the system to recover energy. It stores it in the battery. Many people opt for hybrids because they prioritize eco-friendly transportation. Hybrid cars have lower emissions, but some models switch between electric and gas power. Manufacturers like Toyota began producing hybrid models since these vehicles are gaining popularity. They offer improved fuel efficiency, and some governments offer incentives.

SIMPLE, COMPOUND, AND COMPLEX SENTENCES II STUDENT HANDOUT

Part I: Introduction

Understanding different sentence structures can improve the richness and flow of your writing. There are three main types of sentences: simple, compound, and complex.

- Simple Sentence: Contains one independent clause AND expresses a complete thought.
- Compound Sentence: Contains two or more independent clauses, often joined by a coordinating conjunction and a comma.
- Complex Sentence: Contains an independent clause and one or more dependent clauses, usually joined by subordinating conjunctions.

Part II: Combining Simple Sentences

To create compound sentences, join simple sentences using coordinating conjunctions (F.A.N.B.O.Y.S.) and a comma. For complex sentences, incorporate subordinating conjunctions (e.g., although, because, when) to join independent and dependent clauses.

Part A: Social Media - Paragraph 1 (Simple Sentences)

Social media platforms connect people globally. They allow sharing thoughts, photos, and videos. Users can interact in real time. Social media facilitates communication. Many platforms are available for different purposes. Facebook is popular for networking. Instagram focuses on visual content. Twitter limits posts to 280 characters. TikTok is known for short-form videos. YouTube is a hub for video content.

Directions for Students

1. Underline at least 6 sentences that can be combined.
2. Revise the paragraph to include a variety of simple, complex, and compound sentences.

_____

_____

_____

Part B: Hybrid Vehicles - Paragraph (Simple Sentences)

Hybrid vehicles combine gasoline engines with electric motors. They aim to reduce fuel consumption. These cars use regenerative braking. This system recovers energy. It stores it in the battery. Many people opt for hybrids. They prioritize eco-friendly transportation. Hybrid cars have lower emissions. Some models switch between electric and gas power. Manufacturers like Toyota produce hybrid models. These vehicles are gaining popularity. They offer improved fuel efficiency. Some governments offer incentives.

Directions for Students

1. Underline at least 6 sentences that can be combined.
2. Revise the paragraph to include a variety of simple, complex, and compound sentences.

Revision Directions - Combine the underlined sentences to form compound or complex sentences. Use coordinating conjunctions (F.A.N.B.O.Y.S.) with commas for compound sentences and subordinating conjunctions to create complex sentences.

_____

_____

_____

_____

_____

_____

_____

_____

_____

_____

V for Voice

This element of writing is challenging to teach, and it is essential since it reveals the essence of a writer. It is their tone; it is their way of speaking - the way they use words. Developing a signature voice in writing takes years.

slang	certain phrases that capture their personal way of speaking	personality

P for Presentation

The P refers to presentation. It is the final trait because it is the last aspect a writer needs to consider. Presentation refers to the overall appearance of a piece of writing. It focuses on how well the writing is visually presented, structured, and formatted. There are several elements to consider in presentation

Formatting	This refers to organizing text on the page, including paragraph breaks, headings, and subheadings. Proper formatting helps make the writing easier to read and understand.
Neatness and Legibility	The physical appearance of the writing can also impact its presentation. Neat and legible writing allows readers to understand the words and sentences easily.
Use of Fonts and Formatting Styles	Specific fonts and formatting styles may be required or preferred depending on the context. Following the teacher's guidelines or the writing prompt can contribute to a polished and formal presentation.
Graphics and images	Choose graphics, charts, and other images (or pictures) that can enhance the understanding of the topic. If the writing has statistics and trends, a chart or graphic can be included to illustrate the information. If it is a narrative, pictures or drawings of the characters and setting may be included.

CHAPTER 7
E FOR
ENCOURAGING CREATIVITY

Frame written tasks in a positive way.	If you treat writing like a gift, your child will welcome the challenge.	Remember that if you treat writing like a burden, it will transfer to your child.
Try saying: I have the opportunity I get to …	Avoid negative phrases: I have to … I've got to …	• I am not writing all of that. • I do not know why there is so much writing; I am not reading all that. • Your writing is sloppy. I cannot even read it.

Writing Punishments

Many parents employ the ultimate way to turn a child against writing by making it a negative consequence.

- You cannot leave this room until you write an apology.
- Write "I will not disobey" 500 times.

Other Methods

Remixing well-known stories may include reimagining the story of Goldilocks and the Three Bears. For example, people have already published books written from Mother Bear's, the baby bear's, and Papa Bear's perspective. That creates a whole new story and unleashes their creativity, giving them the creative license to try something new.

Sequel to Goldilocks	Prequel to Goldilocks
How do the three bears react to Goldilocks' thievery? Do they go to Goldilocks' home to report her behavior to her parents? How about the police?	Baby bear and Goldilocks attend the same preschool. The parents could be friends. Some disagreement causes Mama Bear and Goldilocks' mother to stop speaking.

Sequel to Goldilocks	Prequel to Goldilocks
Will Goldilocks repair her damage by volunteering and replacing items in the Bear family's home? How do the families continue to interact after this incident?	Goldilocks' family is a family of thieves who gets this type of behavior from her parents.

Reimagining *Mufaro's Beautiful Daughters*

Switch the tone for each scene	New dialogue
Explore how characters would manifest curiosity, fear, sadness, and anger.	How would their assigned emotion change the actions made during different scenes?

Presentations

Juneteenth Festivities	Independence Day
Family Reunions	Easter Sunday

"EGO TRIPPING" POETRY LESSON + WORKSHEET

Lesson Plan

Created by T.D. Flenaugh, author and host of the Falling for Learning Podcast

Subject: Language Arts - Poetry Analysis

Objective: Students will analyze Nikki Giovanni's poem "Ego Tripping (There may be a Reason Why)" for figurative language and create their own version inspired by the original poem.

Materials:

- Copies of the poem "Ego Tripping (There may be a Reason Why)" by Nikki Giovanni https://poets.org/poem/ego-tripping-there-may-be-reason-why
- Worksheet handouts for each student
- Writing materials

Lesson Outline

Introduction (5 minutes):

1. Introduce the concept of figurative language (hyperbole, allusion, and metaphor).
2. Explain the importance of using figurative language in poetry to evoke imagery and deeper meaning.
3. Introduce Nikki Giovanni as a renowned poet and present her poem "Ego Tripping (There may be a Reason Why)" as today's focus.

First Read Aloud (10 minutes):

1. Ask students to follow along as you read the poem aloud.
2. Encourage them to pay attention to the overall theme and message conveyed in the poem.

Second Read for Figurative Language (15 minutes):

1. Distribute the worksheet handouts to students.
2. Instruct students to reread the poem silently, this time focusing on identifying instances of figurative language like hyperbole, allusions, and repetition.
3. Ask them to annotate the text by underlining examples of figurative language and writing notes explaining the type of figurative language used and its effect on the poem.

Discussion and Analysis (10 minutes):

1. Lead a discussion about the figurative language found in the poem.
2. Have students share their annotations and explanations.
3. Discuss how each type of figurative language contributes to the poem's overall meaning, imagery, and impact on the reader.

Activity 2 - Creating Inspired Poems (20 minutes):

1. Explain that students will now create their own poems inspired by Nikki Giovanni's work.
2. Provide sentence frames based on the structure of the poem's first stanza: "I was born in the congo" will be changed to "I was born _____" for each line.
3. Instruct students to fill in the blanks with their own details, making the poem autobiographical, based on their aspirations, or centered around a character they create.
4. Encourage creativity and experimentation with language while ensuring each line reflects a different aspect of the chosen theme.

Conclusion (5 minutes):

1. Invite volunteers to share their newly created poems with the class.
2. Summarize the lesson by revisiting the importance of figurative language in poetry and how it allows writers to express vivid imagery and deeper emotions.

EGO TRIPPING READING TASK
LESSON WORKSHEET

Directions:

- Re-read the poem to identify five instances of figurative language (hyperbole, allusion, and metaphor). Use the three examples to help you.
- Underline the five examples in the poem. In the margin, label with the type of figurative language.
- Write the five examples below. Make sure to quote the line, explain the type of figurative language used, and its effect on the poem.

Figurative Language Examples in "Ego Tripping":

1. Example 1:

Type of Figurative Language: Hyperbole

Line: "I walked to the fertile crescent and built the sphinx."

Effect: Exaggerates the speaker's power and influence by claiming to have constructed the Sphinx, highlighting a sense of grandiosity.

2. Example 2:

Type of Figurative Language: Allusion

Line: "I gave birth to the sun and nursed him."

Effect: Refers to an allusion of a mythical act, suggesting the speaker's nurturing and life-giving abilities.

3. Example 3:

Type of Figurative Language: Repetition

Line: "I turned myself into myself and was Jesus."

Effect: Emphasizes the idea of self-realization and transformation through the repetition of the phrase "I turned myself into myself."

NAME:_____ **DATE:** _____

4.

Type of Figurative Language: _____

Line: _____

Effect: _____

5.

Type of Figurative Language: _____

Line: _____

Effect: _____

6.

Type of Figurative Language: _____

Line: _____

Effect: _____

7.

Type of Figurative Language: _____

Line: _____

Effect: _____

8.

Type of Figurative Language: _____

Line: _____

Effect: _____

NAME:_____   DATE: _____

WRITING TASK
BORROWING FROM THE MASTER

Use the poem "Ego Tripping" as a mentor text to develop a poem. Use the lines as a frame to create a poem that is autobiographical, aspirational, or in the voice of a character of your choosing.

Here are some examples:

Original Lines	**Frames**
I was born in the congo I walked to the fertile crescent and built the sphinx	I was born _____ I walked _____ And _____
I designed a pyramid so tough that a star that only glows every one hundred years falls into the center giving divine perfect light I am bad	I designed _____ So tough that _____ Giving divine perfect light I am bad

Autobiographical Example

I was born in Pomona

I walked to the corner store for candy promised and bought the meat grandma requested

Aspirational Example

I designed a book

So tough that screenwriters fought over it and tore a page from the center

It glowed giving divine perfect light

I am bad

Challenge

Use new word choices to make the poem your own. Instead of walked, what other synonyms can be used?

_____

_____

Instead of "I am bad", what other terms can be used?

_____

_____

Instead of "divine perfect light" what else can illustrate how awesome or powerful something is?

_____

_____

Writing Prompt

Create a 20 line poem with at least 4 stanzas that includes four (4) uses of figurative language. Focus the poem on an autobiographical account, an aspiration (goal), or a character of your choice.

_____

_____

_____

_____

_____

_____

NAME:_____ **DATE:** _____

_____

_____

_____

_____

_____

_____

_____

_____

_____

_____

_____

_____

_____

_____

_____

_____

_____

_____

SAMPLE ASSIGNMENT SHEET
WHERE THE RED FERN GROWS CULMINATING
WRITING ASSIGNMENT

You have a choice of three assignments that you can do to celebrate the end of the novel. Choose one of the following tasks.

A) Write a letter + Draw an Illustration

Pretend that you are Billy. Write a letter to one of the following characters: Grandpa, Rubin, Mother, Father, Old Dan, or Little Ann. In a **four-paragraph** letter. explain how you feel about a conflict that involves the chosen character in the book: grateful to them, sympathy towards them, respect or admiration for them, or whatever emotion you choose. Use at least three events in the novel that involve Billy and the chosen character to provide evidence for the emotions in the letter.

Include a drawing of Billy with the other character detailing one of the scenes in the book.

B) Write an essay

In a **6-paragraph essay**, analyze one of the following characters: Billy, Little Ann, Old Dan, or Grandpa's character or personality. Choose four events in the novel that show this character's personality. Explain how each of these events shaped the novel and the character.

C) Write a narrative poem + Conduct a reading

Choose three events from the novel. Create **three** (3) narrative poems of twenty lines each that detail the happening within each of these events. Be sure to include rising action, climax, falling action, and a resolution. For each poem use at least three metaphors and two similes. The poem **must** rhyme.

In addition, you must read one page of the novel from one of these events in front of the class. You will be scored on how you read aloud with expression, appropriate pacing, and the ability for the audience to hear and understand you.

DUE DATES

Date to Choose topic: _____

Date Brainstorm/Outline due: _____

Date Rough draft is due: _____

Date Final Draft is due: _____

NAMES ESSAY

We will discuss and read about many types of names: at-home names, first names, last names, middle names, nicknames, and titles. Think about your names and the types of names you have.

You will write an essay about one of your names, **or** you can choose to write about a few of your names. <u>You may also write about someone else's name.</u>

You should:

☐ Provide origin/meaning information about the name or names.

☐ Explain how the name(s) was chosen or given.

☐ Provide information about cultures, languages, or naming traditions that relate to the name(s).

☐ Describe feelings about the name(s).

☐ Include an introduction paragraph and a conclusion paragraph.

OUTLINING/PLANNING THE NAMES ESSAY

After discussion and listing, narrow down your ideas.

CHOOSE - three aspects of your name that you will write about (first, middle, last, nickname(s)...)

For each name, you should be able to list at least three facts.

NAMES BRAINSTORM HANDOUT

Family names, traditions	Titles	Nicknames from friends	Mean nicknames	Name changes
Mispronunciations	Sensory details looks, smells, tastes	Jokes about names	Reminds you of...	Culture/language

Write anything else that may come to mind about your name.

_____

_____

_____

_____

_____